Critical Infrastructure for Children

The Astonishing Potential of New England Schools

Questions and Answers on How New England Education can Create Opportunities for Everyone

Matthew J. Fraser

SALEM
HOUSE
PRESS

Salem House Press

PO Box 249

Salem MA 01970

Copyright @ 2017, 2022, 2024 by Matthew J. Fraser

 ISBN-10: 0-9862610-6-8

 ISBN-13: 978-0-9862610-6-0

Library of Congress Number: 2017937690

First Edition 2017

Acadia National Park, Bar Harbor, Maine

Above: Acadia National Park in Bar Harbor, Maine, something all young people in New England should experience.

Matthew J. Fraser has been teaching and studying
languages since 1995. He maintains a website at:
www.thelanguageguy.net

Contents

Question Sections

Introduction

Dear Readers,

Critical Infrastructure for Children is a collection of two hundred and fifteen questions and answers, all with one focus: to act as a mini-almanac of New England education, designed for parents, students and educators. The book could also be used by anyone else interested in learning more about existing successful models, at local schools and colleges.

In late 1997, I came home from abroad to begin writing and preparing for what I believed was coming: a time of true crisis. After reading a variety of reports and writing in notebooks for a few months, I came across the MassINC., report *The State of the American Dream in Massachusetts (1996)*, as it was around the house. I recognized that this report, and other reports by MassINC. contained much needed foundational principles, and by the fall of 2000 the four educational principles were established. Those principle were: the need for more vocational education, quality physical education, quality language learning programs and the need to teach personal finance. Since then, I have worked *every day* in some way, including reading and writing or taking challenging teaching jobs that informed my writing.

You can see the work in the text, footnotes, Bibliography and Index. I encourage readers to challenge book ideas to create even better ideas and solutions – in fact – I DARE YOU. (1) And yes, that was the sound of the gauntlet being thrown - ENJOY!

Matthew J. Fraser

* * *

1. The quote "I DARE YOU" is from the 2012 movie Detropia , which profiled the complete collapse of Detroit. The quote was from a scene in which a girl was walking through an abandoned, once proud music hall, where great, glorious symphonies were played in the Motor City, the city that was the center of the U.S. auto industry. That past was contrasted with the girl's present, in which she was walking through an abandoned, decrepit music hall. As she crept through the music hall with a head lamp and flashlight, she spoke to her dreams of Detroit making a comeback. In that talk, she spoke to those who might choose to step up and make a difference, and said "I DARE YOU". The truth is that those words inspired me to change the tone of this book a bit, and to speak more honestly and directly to readers in the introduction. This book is, in practice, a response to those words.

Detropia (2012) 1h 30m. Directed by: Heidi Ewing and Rachel Grady. Official Description: *"A documentary on the city of Detroit and its woes, which are emblematic of the U.S. and the collapse of its manufacturing base."* m.IMDb.com

* * *

People have provided you with the opportunities for a fine education, it is time to pay it forward. Plus if done right, those students may graduate and make our society a better place to live.

How to Read this Book

This book is packed with information, some of which you may be interested in, and some of which you may not be. For maximum satisfaction, you may want to browse the Table of Contents to find an area of special interest. It's up to you, but this is a supremely practical book, so you should use it however works best for you.

Cover to Cover versus Reading by Section

You may choose to read this book cover to cover, but there is so much information to process, that this is not for everyone. That said, you could learn an enormous of amount in doing so. Then again, you may enjoy reading one section at a time to find what you need, then to go to the Internet to expand your learning and or even begin developing your ideas.

Reading by Index

Another way to read this book is to thumb through the Index and find a subject, author or person of interest – and research away! I encourage you to use this book to start your own rabbit hole journey: let something spark your interest or curiosity and go to the internet or your favorite influencers on the internet and social media and learn more. The more you learn, the more you will be able to do to make more options for today's youth.

For Sources Highlighted in CIC

Book sources can find their work in footnotes, Bibliography, or Index. I would encourage sources to read other parts of the book – even if only to understand the context of your reference in this book. I also encourage sources to learn about the other sources that relate to their work, and perhaps even reach out to them – engagement is key in collaborating for lasting solutions! This could be extremely healthy for everyone – after all, if we're going to make New England the best place it can possibly be, we're going to need to connect, listen, learn, and perhaps – gasp – even work together.

How Parents, Students and Educators Can Read This Book

A Resource for Students and Parents

Parents and students can use this book as a resource to create opportunities and make the best possible choices in education. In fact this is exactly what we need; a whole new generation of students on college campuses sinking their teeth into these questions and coming up with their own answers.

The million dollar question, or rather the two million job question, is how to save the 2 million manufacturing jobs that UMass Lowell President stated that we are at risk of losing in the next ten years. (1)

A Resource for Future Authors

Many of the 200+ questions in this book could be the subject of an entire, useful book, and I encourage others to step up to the plate to do the hard research and writing. Conservation, K-12 education, progressive college coursework, physical education for the disabled, farm job creation, enriching the lives of children; these are all themes that require exploration in full books.

New England Schools and Colleges

Although there is rivalry and competition between schools, everyone benefits as we listen and learn from each other, especially students. When some refer to "investment in infrastructure" some are referring to roads and bridges, but I emphasize the development of our educational system to develop the workforce and critical thinkers for the next generation.

* * *

1. Dan O'Brien, *The Lowell Sun,* "UML Christens Partnership for Workforce Development" UMass Lowell. www.uml.edu/News/news-articles/2015/sun-massmep.aspx

* * *

What You Can do After Reading This Book

Whereas the questions in the book represent information that parents, students and educators should have, the following are some successes you can learn more about now. They are here because they are the future, and always in motion.

A. The University of Texas Social Security Course Model One Social Security course at the University of Texas extension school looks at the 82 pathways to entry into Social Security. Choosing the right path of entry can make all the difference for the program that impacts almost half of American households. (2)

B. Social Security Sustainability According to the *Portland Press Herald (3),* Social Security may have funding issues as soon as 2030. For the 70 million Americans currently in the program, and for the next 70 million, we need to watch the Social Security Trust Fund.

See: ssa.gov/policy/social-security-long-term-financial-outlook.html

C. Deferred Maintenance and Federal Interest Rates A big issue facing public colleges today; massive deferred maintenance. (4) You can learn about those specific maintenance needs. To survive, many New England schools depend on funding. However, with federal interest payments scheduled to rise to over one trillion dollars a year by 2030, federal funding for schools will be *bitterly contested. (5)*

To read the report on the future of federal interest payments and more, see: "An Update to the Budget Outlook: 2023 to 2033, published in May of 2023 by the Congressional Budget Office. See also: "Federal Net Interest Payments on page 82.

D. Vocational Schools Help assure that young people looking to learn a trade can do so. One dimension of understanding the value of vocational schools is to see the list of skills recognized by the Articulation Agreements on page 85.

E. Teaching Personal Finance The most successful model for teaching personal finance is profiled in questions 155-157: that of the Salem State economics department, as they have succeeded in every dimension of how to convey this critical knowledge.

* * *

2. "Maximizing Social Security", University of Texas Extension School.
3. Davison, Laura Bloomberg ""Virus Could Deplete Social Security Funds by 2030, Report Says." *Portland Press Herald.* October 22, 2020 www.pressherald.com
4. Krantz, Laura, "Backlog on building upkeep is mounting at state campuses", *The Boston Globe.* www.bostonglobe.com/ 05/29/2017
5. "An Update to the Budget Outlook: 2023 to 2033, Congressional Budget Office, May 2023. For more detail on the role different dimensions of interest costs, and an explanation of the historical context, see also: "Federal Net Interest Costs: A Primer," published in December of 2020 by the Congressional Budget Office.

* * *

F. The Articulation Agreements It is important to know about the role that the 2011 Articulation Agreements play and how vocational skills certificates are recognized in the community college system, at state four year colleges and elsewhere. (6) See the list of skills recognized by the Articulation Agreements on page 85.

G. Learn About Credit Transfer Systems One dimension of understanding the public and private college system is to learn about the credit transfer systems. The way in which credits can be transferred has changed and so have the tools for doing so. In Massachusetts, this website is MassTransfer, which also contains information about the A2B program and the Commonwealth Commitment.

In New Hampshire, the website of NH Transfer allows visitors to see how community college credits transfer to bachelor degrees at the New Hampshire state colleges, Keene St. and Plymouth St.

In Maine, the "Transfer Equivalencies" page show how courses move from colleges in the Maine Community College system to the University of Maine.

The "Transfer from CCV" page outlines how to transfer credits from the Community College of Vermont to state colleges. That page also outlines the "Special Transfer" agreements between the community colleges and specific colleges.

In Rhode Island, the "Transfer Evaluation system" page demonstrates how to move credits from the multiple campuses of the Community College of Rhode Island to Rhode Island College and URI.

In Connecticut, the University of Connecticut has the "Transfer Course from CT Institutions page is responsible for credit transfer evaluation, which allows students to gain credits toward a four year degree at the affordable community colleges.

* * *

6. Massachusetts State Articulation Agreement Between Massachusetts Community Colleges and Massachusetts Chapter 74 Approved Secondary Career/Vocational Technical Programs, Massachusetts Community Colleges. www.masscc.org/sites/default/files/Engineering.pdf The link here is one of many articulation agreements between vocational schools and New England community colleges.

* * *

Job Creation

A. Industry Partnerships with Community Colleges Industry partnerships with community colleges near them can be a path to employment. GPSTEM initiatives are one example, which stands for "Guided Pathways to Success in Science, Technology, Engineering and Mathematics." (7) Maybe you can find better models by exploring the sites of the schools on the map on pages 73 and 90.

B. STEM There is a lot to understand about STEM jobs and coursework, which is why pages 114-118 focus exclusively on that. Standing for Science, Technology, Engineering and Math, STEM fields represent a significant amount of future jobs.

C. New England Apprenticeship Programs Colleges like Vermont Technical College and York County Community College are leading the way with new approaches to connecting workers to apprenticeships in the trades. You can find out how they work and learn about any in your area. Page 89 has a list of existing apprenticeships, but more may be added in the time to come.

D. Support the Disabled, Support the Economy Tools for supporting the disabled while supporting everyone are on pages 98-101.

E. MEP Trainings Each of the six New England states has a Manufacturing Extension Partnership, which supports manufacturing and the creation of manufacturing jobs. One program are seven week, 280 hour seminars to teach the basics of CNC. (Computer Numerical Control) After training, workers have become qualified manufacturing workers that manufacturers are desperate to find. (8)

F. Support Adjunct Professors Adjunct professors represent the microcosm of the suffering working class; they work incredibly hard and contribute a great deal, yet they are often treated poorly and suffer in poverty. You can check out the proposed responses on page 31.Supporting them is supporting us.

G. The Two Million Job Challenge Jacqueline Moloney, President of University of Massachusetts Lowell said: "*Over the next decade, nearly 3.5 million manufacturing jobs will likely need to be filled, and the skills gap is expected to result in 2 million of those jobs going unfilled.*" One article that spoke to the support of community colleges, which is one of many dimensions of this, is below. (9)

* * *

7. "Guided Pathways to Success in STEM", Greenfield Community College. masscc.org/partnerships-initiatives/guided-pathways-success-stem
8. Kathie Mahoney, MassMEP Partners with UMass Lowell to Expand Advanced CNC Training in Massachusetts, https://massmep.org/massmep-partners-with-umass-lowell-to-.../
9. Derek Z. Jackson, "If Colleges Had An Extra 200 million", *The Boston Globe*, September 3, 2015.
* * *

Quality of Life

Youth Brain Health Football, women's hockey and other sports programs struggle with the brain injury and CTE or chronic traumatic encephalopathy issue. (10) Great work in this field is being done at the University of New Hampshire. See "Helmetless Tackling Research at UNH", on their youtube channel for how their work can make sports safer.

Grandmother's Colleges In the trailer of *The Economics of Happiness,* in which an older woman spoke of the need to start "grandmother's colleges", because that is the only way to assure that local knowledge never dies. (11) One way to do this is within existing colleges, such as The Explorers Club at Salem State in MA.

The "Conservation Participation Rate" To effectively respond to the challenge of preserving the environment for the generations to come, then we need more people involved in conservation. For starters, we can study the goals of Regional Conservation partnerships, (RCPs) and find ways to collaborate with university departments. (12) Another, easy way to participate is to watch the movie The American Serengeti, a movie narrated by Tom Selleck that imagines a new national park in the midwest.

Fight Species Extinction Species are dying every day, in part because conservation biology (CB) courses "teach students about the issue of extinction without giving them the tools to fight it". Shifting from passive study to problem-solving the problem is a step in the right direction. (13)

* * *

10. "Helmetless Tackling Research at UNH", Youtube video, University of New Hampshire. www.youtube.com/watch?v=4Y24z6_orRs

11. *The Economics of Happiness.* www.youtube.com/watch?v=VkdnFYDbiBE
12. The RCP Network - Overview, Wildlands and Woodlands. www.wildlandsandwoodlands.org/rcpnetwork
13. Moyer-Horner, Lucas "Education as a tool for addressing the extinction crisis: moving students from understanding to action". PubMed.

* * *

Critical Infrastructure for Children
The Astonishing Potential of New England Schools

Questions and Answers on How New England
Education can Create Opportunities for Everyone

♦

"Well, if you want to sing out, sing out

And if you want to be free, be free

'Cause there's a million things to be

You know that there are"

- Cat Stevens, Harold and Maude

This beautiful quote from the movie *Harold and Maude* may seem idealistic and perhaps even unrealistic to some, but the truth is that there are a million great, different ways for the people of New England to live their lives. However, for this to unfold in a way that works for everyone and is sustainable for the generations to come, we're going to need to put our heads together and look at all dimensions of this bright dream of the future.

The first twelve questions in this book represent not only the core principles of the book, but also the themes that the ten sections of the work explore in greater depth. So, without further ado, on to the questions.

One of the few state colleges that Massachusetts has lost
in recent years. We need to make sure we do not lose any
more which could prevent the middle class from providing their children an education. Highlighting their existing and their effective programs is the focus of this book.

1-12:

Top Questions in Education to Answer for the People of New England

"The average American school now has one guidance counselor for every 500 students. In some places the ratio is far more dire — nearly 1,000 kids for every counselor....I think it's a massive crisis...I think it's really the black hole in the American education system."

Bill Symonds, director of Global Pathways Institute, to WBUR's Robin Young

1. What is the number one change young people need in Massachusetts education? Greater utilization of vocational education. Currently in Massachusetts, only seven percent of students attend vocational schools, although the research of MassINC. has led me to believe that thirty to forty percent of students would be better off in vocational programs. (1) The first issue with the present situation is that too many of the thirty to forty percent of the students who should be in a vocational program graduate from high school with a traditional education, that doesn't open the doors it once did.

The trend in recent years has been of America splitting into two halves; the haves and the have-nots, and it's important to use vocational education to give young people skills they need to thrive in our global economy. Combine skills with teaching personal finance and we can give students the tools they need to survive and thrive.

Another effect of under utilized vocational education is that both teaching and learning are often difficult in a class of thirty when ten to twelve students shouldn't or don't want to be there. So, why not let more students discover if carpentry or electrical work is for them? The choice of high school program should not simply be a matter of conformity.

Combining Traditional and Vocational Studies

The State of the American Dream by MassINC states that not only would thirty to forty percent of students be better off in a vocational high school, but as many as half would be better off with a combination of traditional and vocational programming. (2) In 2005, when *Ideas for America: New Hope Rises* came out, one challenge facing vocational schools was parental pressure; many simply wanted their kids to go to college. However, since the MassINC. report *The State of the American Dream,* (1996) there has been an increase in vocational school applications and community colleges have responded to needs in the work force. (3)

* * *

1. Edward Moscovitch, Closing the Gap: Raising Skills to Raise Wages (Boston: MassINc., 1997), Executive Summary
2. Ibid.
3.Edwin L. Aguirre, "MassMEP, UMass Lowell Address New Workforce Training Program", November 03, 2015. www.uml.edu/News/stories/2015/Workforce-development-partnership.aspx

* * *

4

With regards to rising applications to vocational schools, the increased interest in them may be a response to the declining stability within the country and thus increased value placed upon skilled labor employment opportunities.

Vocational Education and Articulation Agreements

Community colleges in New England have responded to the need for vocational education in a variety of highly effective and innovative ways. This includes the State-wide Articulation Agreement in Massachusetts in 2012, which allows vocational school students to receive college credit at the community colleges in Massachusetts for certificates received. What this means is that vocational school students now have one more powerful tool; their connection with these community colleges means that students and parents can now more clearly see the road to a successful career. Additionally, students can often transfer credit from community colleges to state colleges, which is explained on pages 90 to 91.

2. How does greater utilization of vocational programs relate to responding to the need for skilled workers? Vocational education can help prepare students for further education, in part because certificates received at vocational schools can be redeemed for credit at community colleges.(4) The issue is, only seven percent of Massachusetts students are in vocational programs, although according to a 1996 MassINC. report that number should be around thirty to forty percent, with as many as fifty percent doing a combination of the classical and vocational studies.

Students can receive training in manufacturing at different colleges in New England with or without a vocational background, but the fact that under utilized vocational education coincides with the fact that New England manufacturers can't find needed skilled workers seems to be a reflection of a flaw in our culture. In short, educational snobbery is getting in the way and we need to correct this.

York County CC President Finkelstein Speaks

Perhaps one of the best articles on the role of education in responding to needs in New England manufacturing was written by Barbara Finkelstein, then president of York County Community College. Her November 19, 2016 article in the *Portland Press Herald* "Maine Voices; Manufacturing's Best Days Might Still be to Come", emphasizes the role that community colleges in Maine are play in providing the training young people need.

"It's not just that manufacturing contributes so much to our local economy in southern Maine, it creates more than 18 million jobs nationally and comprises roughly 12 percent of our gross domestic product. It's that the sector has evolved so seamlessly into the modern workplace, where companies employ state-of-the-art technologies to deliver the best products in the world more quickly and with higher quality than ever." (5)

* * *

4. Ibid.
5. Barbara Finkelstein, "Maine Voices, Maine Voices; Manufacturing's Best Days Might Be Yet to Come", *Portland Press Herald,* November 19th, 2016.

* * *

(According to Salary.com, the average starting salary of a manufacturing engineer is $71,000) (6)

In her piece in the *Portland Press Herald*, President Finkelstein outlined the potential of a bright future for manufacturing in Maine and also pointed out that the manufacturing jobs of the present are not the gritty, filthy factories of centuries past, but rather clean, safe environments.

3. What are manufacturing groups telling us about the job market as it relates to the need of schools to respond? We need skilled workers. According to the Massachusetts Manufacturing Extension Partnership:

"*Massachusetts is facing a critical shortfall in skilled workers, with jobs currently unfilled and more expected to open up over the next ten years. Competition for skilled workers and employees, with just the most basic skills, is and will continue to keep companies from growing.*" (7)

75,000 Jobs for New England? Readers might have a look at the ways that the University of Massachusetts at Lowell and other New England colleges are responding to the lack of a skilled workforce, as according to my calculations, we are at risk of losing up to 80,000 jobs within New England. If the quote below says that we are at risk of losing 2 million jobs, and New England makes up about four percent of the national population, then I four percent of 3 million jobs is about 120,000.

According to an article on December 12, 2013 by Jay Fitzgerald of the *Boston Globe*, Massachusetts has lots of positions that simply can't be filled. (8) A November 2012 *60 Minutes* show on CBS echoed the same grim reality, with an article titled "3 Million Jobs Nationally, but Who's Qualified." (9)

"*The manufacturing industry is facing a critical shortfall in skilled workers, with jobs currently unfilled and more expected to open up within the next ten years...Moloney cited a recent report that projects that over the next decade, nearly 3.5 million jobs will likely need to be filled, and the skills gap is expected to result in 2 million of those jobs going unfilled.*" (10)

"*Within Massachusetts, as many as 25,000 manufacturing jobs will go unfilled in the next five years, due to the lack in the number of people qualified*". (11)

* * *

6. Salary.com

7. Dan O'Brien, "UML Christens Parnership for Workforce Development", Lowell Sun, from the UMass Lowell website, December 5, 2015. www.uml.edu/

8. Fitzgerald, Jay, "Worker's Skills aren't Matching Available Jobs," The Boston Globe, December 15, 2013. www.bostonglobe.com/

9. "Three Million Jobs in U.S., But Who's Qualified?", November 11, 2012, CBS News. www.cbsnews.com/

10. Jay Fitzgerald, "Worker's Skills Aren't Matching Available Jobs", The Boston Globe, December 17, 2013. www.northeastern.edu/

11. The Future of Work in Massachusetts. page 15, edited by Tom Juravich.

* * *

Ideally, vocational educators will be kept updated on the needs of the manufacturing sector and be able to adjust accordingly. The good news is that at community, state and flagship colleges in New England are responding to this situation: see question 133 for more on that. (12)

4. What is the most important piece of knowledge young people will need to navigate the world? Understanding the basics of personal finance, including mortgages, financing, renting and credit. In my experience, young people desperately need this knowledge but are not getting it. I emphasize this from both my own experience and listening to students talk about their future, and hearing the lack of certainty and understanding. I was twenty-eight years old before I had this knowledge and it was only then that saving meant much to me.

As a high school teacher, I was a little surprised to find that almost zero of my students understood the basics of a mortgage, but as a graduate student I was surprised to find that very few of the college students understood mortgages either.

If a young person is working or trying to choose a trade, it is important to know not only how much money he will earn in that trade, but also what is possible to do with that money and skills acquired. If a student knows that by becoming a carpenter he might earn $40,000 a year, and also understands how mortgages work, he can imagine what sort of house and lifestyle he might afford on that wage.

Training High School Teachers There are many ways to communicate this knowledge to young people, including auditorium presentations, classroom presentations and as part of the curriculum. Auditorium presentations are by far the most affordable, although integrating the study of mortgages, financing, renting and credit into math class is another approach. The Salem State economics department trains teachers on how to teach personal finance, and questions 155-157 focus on that.

5. What is the role of adult education in New England and how have community colleges responded? Adult education has come a long way. In my 2005 book *Ideas for America,* the basics of adult education were broken down into three main categories; teaching workers English, remedial skills and some community based courses for fun. However, with the rise of distance learning, apprenticeships, industry partnership, eight week trainings in CNC (Computer Numerical Control) through the MEPs and the ease in which credits can be transferred from community to state colleges, the ability of community colleges to create employment within New England has grown.

* * *

12. This end note could cite many programs at New England community colleges that are leading to employment, but the success of Vermont Technical college is particularly striking. Offering two and four year programs at multiple locations throughout Vermont, graduates of Vermont Technical College has 100% of its students hired upon graduation. In fact, it was the work of VTC that inspired me to look closely at innovation at community colleges in New England, which greatly influenced the book you hold in your hand.

www.vtc.edu/news/vermont-tech-class-2016-reports-100-placement-rate

* * *

Another change is that Vermont and Massachusetts offer credit programs for high school students. In Massachusetts, this is drawn out by the state Articulation Agreement of 2012 (13), whereas in Vermont this is part of the Pathways to Progress program. (14)

6. What should the public be mindful of with regard to public colleges in New England? Prices, quality of programming, the development of the industry partnerships, apprenticeships and other programs at the community colleges. Another aspect should be an awareness of the roles of the three dimensions of the public college system; the community colleges, the state colleges (now mostly universities) and the flagship colleges for each state. Things are moving fast, and in recent years I believe there has been a blurring of the lines of their roles.

You may prefer going to the website of one community college, but I enjoy going through the New England Community College Website Portals below.

Connecticut: ct.edu
Maine: mccs.me.edu
Massachusetts: masscc.org
New Hampshire: ccsnh.edu
Rhode Island: ccri.edu
Vermont: ccv.edu

Pockets of Excellence Not only do public colleges still represent some of the most affordable options in New England, but they have pockets of great excellence in certain departments and programs. For example, the old teacher's colleges tend to have strong programs in education, whereas Lyndon State in Vermont is said to have had a great meteorology department. Perhaps greater public understanding of these "pockets of excellence" will help when advocating for funding to the most affordable institutions of higher learning. (15)

State College versus Flagship College

I think a lot of people don't understand the difference between a state university and the flagship universities, or at least I know I didn't. In Vermont, the University of Vermont is the state "flagship" university, whereas in Massachusetts, the "flagship college" is the University of Massachusetts with its main campus in Amherst. There is also UMass Boston, UMass Dartmouth, UMass Worcester (Medical School) and UMass Lowell, which are branches of the flagship colleges.

* * *

13. Massachusetts State Articulation Agreement Between Massachusetts Community Colleges and Massachusetts Chapter 74 Approved Secondary Career/Vocational Technical Programs, Massachusetts Community Colleges. www.masscc.org/sites/default/files/Engineering.pdf. The link here is one of many articulation agreements between vocational schools and New England community colleges.
14. "Pathways for High School Students". Vermont State Colleges.
15. "Tuition and Mandatory Fees at Massachusetts Public Colleges and Universities". www.mass.edu/datacenter/tuition/appendixtuitionfeesweight7.asp
* * *

The State Colleges It can be confusing to say "state colleges", because in a way the state colleges (now mostly universities) are more like regional colleges. I noticed that Vermont Technical College refers to itself as a regional college, although this reference is seldom used at other state colleges. If you look at a map of the state colleges in Massachusetts you'll see that they serve one region of the state. Westfield St. is in the southwestern part of Massachusetts, MCLA (formerly North Adams State (16)) serves the northwest, Bridgewater St. serves the south shore of Boston, and the other seven colleges serve their region.

The Good Old Days When my Aunt Grace attended Salem State back in the 1940's, life was simpler and regional colleges were affordable. However, with the closure of Hyannis State College (17) and Boston State(18), the conversion of Lowell State into UMass Lowell(19), and North Adams State changing its name to MCLA, I worry that the existence of affordable, high quality colleges is threatened.

Memories of Old Boston I'm particularly aware of Boston State because when I was a sixie (seventh grader) at Boston Latin in the Fall of 1983, the sign on the building of the old Boston State was around the corner from Boston Latin. Our headmaster had gone there, and it was reputedly a fine school. However, today, very few people even know that it once existed, as the old campus has become part of UMass Boston. However, the University of Massachusetts Boston has also been hard hit with budget cuts, with the college in danger of laying off almost a third of its faculty in 2016. I mention that as it seems like a "teachable moment" about the ongoing struggles at all levels of the public college system. (20)

The Vermont State College System Within Vermont, the old state colleges are represented by Johnson State, Castleton State and Lyndon State, although in 2018 Johnson State and Lyndon State merged to form Northern Vermont University. (21) In 2023, those colleges and Vermont Technical College unified under a common accreditation as Vermont State University.

Later in this book you will see a discussion of programs in the Economics departments of Salem State and Bridgewater State, because I believe that the "pockets of excellence" found in individual departments is what will add value to state colleges.

* * *

16. "Our History", Massachusetts College of Liberal Arts. www.mcla.edu/About_MCLA/mission/history/index

17. Hyannis State Teacher's College, America's Lost Colleges. www.lostcolleges.com/hyannis-state-teachers

18. "Boston State", America's Lost Colleges. www.lostcolleges.com/boston-state-college

19. History, UMass Lowell, https://www.uml.edu/Education/About/History.aspx

20. "400 UMass Boston Adjuncts are told Contracts May Not be Renewed", The Boston Globe, June 2, 2016. www.bostonglobe.com/

21. "Northern Vermont University", Lyndon State College.
 http://lyndonstate.edu/about/northern-vermont-university/

* * *

Articulation Agreements

The Statewide Articulation Agreements of Massachusetts are agreements throughout by which graduates of vocational schools can receive credit at a community college and continue their education. (22) The Massachusetts agreements and the various colleges are profiled on page 86, although I would recommend that parents and students dedicate time to learning about the many different articulation agreements in New England that affect them.

For a long time, manufacturing companies have been saying that they have some excellent paying jobs, but that they can't find the people qualified to do the work. The good news is that the University of New Hampshire (23), the University of Maine and many other community and state colleges now offer training in different kinds of manufacturing. (24) See page 133 for more information on the opportunities in manufacturing.

Apprenticeships Another dimension of work being done at regional and state colleges are the apprenticeship programs, by which students can work and go to class over a period of years and acquire a solid skill in a trade. Some of these programs are new and changing rapidly, which is another reason to do research about them.

The work of Vermont Technical College impressed me particularly, which is featured in question 131. York County Community College offers an apprenticeship program (25) that the president of that college has written. In my opinion, the best op-ed in the *Portland Press Herald* about the future of manufacturing in Maine that it's president has written. (26) That said, three apprenticeships that caught my attention the most were at;

* * *

22. The Massachusetts Community Colleges Executive Office (MCCEO) and the State Universities Council of Presidents joined together to answer a call from the Department of Higher Education's Task Force on Collaboration and Efficiency. The councils are comprised of twenty-four PACE, or Partnership to Advance Collaboration & Efficiency, with charter members, including fifteen community colleges and nine state universities, who oversee the Articulation Agreements for the state.
23. There are many public colleges responding to the need for trained workers in manufacturing, but the John Olson Manufacturing Center at College of Engineering and Physical Sciences at the UnIversity of New Hampshire, is one. The John Olson Center "aims to serve as a pipeline for trained, skilled workers who will be able to successfully step into the state's manufacturing sector with practical knowledge and experience". See: ceps.unh.edu/olsoncenter
24. The Advanced Manufacturing Center at the University of Maine is one public college responding to the needs of manufacturers and people looking for a career. "The core mission of the center is to assist manufacturers reach their goals. The core strategies of the AMC are; engineering, research, manufacturing and support services, and to serve as a pipeline for trained, skilled workers who will be able to successfully step into the state's manufacturing sector with practical knowledge and experience." See: umaine.edu/amc/about/
25. York County Community College Apprenticeship program. www.yccc.edu/press_release/pratt-whitney-employees-complete-apprenticeship-program-2/
26. Barbara Finkelstein, "Maine Voices; Manufacturing's Best Days Might Be Yet to Come", *Portland Press Herald*, November 19th, 2016

* * *

Great Bay Community College Shipyard program
Vermont Technical College Electrical and Plumbing Apprenticeships
York County Community College Plumbing Apprenticeship

I ask how community college apprenticeship programs could work in Boston, and if the principle of creating apprenticeships would work. According to an administrator I spoke to at Vermont Technical College, many employers were initially hesitant to take on apprentices, but soon saw that it was worth it for them. (27) See page 89 for a list of existing New England apprenticeships.

Commuters and Public Colleges

Another facet of the state colleges to consider is their special relationship with commuters. The articulation agreements, manufacturing programs and apprenticeship programs are all for commuters, too. The state colleges were set up to be within commuting distance of everyone, which is why you can be anywhere in Massachusetts and not too far from any of them. Within New England, we might consider identifying the "pockets of excellence" within them, and exploring how their work can help as many people as possible, including commuters.

7. What is the appropriate role of testing in language learning? It can be a great tool to assess what has been learned, but it's only one tool. When we talk about Americans learning a foreign language, we're talking about a skill that is nice to have, but when talking about recent immigrants we're talking about acquiring an absolutely necessary skill. What that means to me is tests are only useful if they help recent arrivals acquire a skill.

The Principles of Questions 47-85 Many tactics for improving language programs are outlined in questions 47-86, but for me the number one thing I emphasize, without question, is the value of reading out loud, with emotion.

High Stakes Testing and the Angry Mother Bear

As for responding to the needs of those with physical or mental handicaps, I want to tell a story about an angry mother. Once, I was asked by a mother with a learning disabled daughter if I was in favor of the Massachusetts Comprehensive Assessment System, or MCAS, (28) a Massachusetts test that students must pass to graduate. I said yes; at that time I thought they were a good tool for raising standards. The mother then looked me dead in the eyes and yelled at me, telling me how cruel it was for her learning disabled daughter to not receive a diploma after having gone to high school every day and tried her best, only because she wasn't up to passing the test. The truth of the matter is I just had to listen, because I really had no answer for her.

* * *

27. Vermont Technical College. "Vermont Technical College reports 100% placement rate". www.vtc.edu/news/vermont-tech-class-2016-reports-100-placement-rate
28. Wikipedia, MCAS. http://en.wikipedia.org/wiki/Massachusetts _Comprehensive_Assessment_System

* * *

Terminology

Subject Assessment Tests Subject assessment tests test the knowledge of a specific subject area, such as Math, Science, English or Spanish. Whereas in an A, a B, or a C in a specific subject doesn't guarantee as much as it used to, and these "SAT2s" can give students a chance to demonstrate their knowledge.

Minimum Standards Tests MSTs are generally pass/fail tests, because in order to raise standards there has to be a standard. As a teacher I would prefer such a test, because it doesn't put unnecessary pressure on students; they only need to pass.

Tracking In a college Adolescent Psychology course (necessary for certification) I learned about the system of tracking, whereby students are put in lower level courses, where they often work alone with worksheets. My professor suggested that once students are put in the lower levels, they tend to stay there. (29) After watching the movie *A Place at the Table*, (30) I was alerted to the fact that many children go to school hungry. Tests should show how much has been learned, but only if they're fed and empowered with the best possible learning tools.

Physical Exercise and Language Learning

One of the wilder ideas I came up with to teach languages was combining a language class with physical exercise creating a kind of circuit training, with four minute rounds of reading out loud, followed by four minutes of exercise, so students (especially physical boys and girls) could relax and get healthy at the same time. However, I realize that the implementation could be complicated and so I would emphasize exploring other ways of getting exercise, including:

> *Safe Routes Programs*
> *Implementation of Pedestrian, Bike and Information Center*
> *Maximizing Physical Education*

8. How can progressive school and college coursework lead to opportunities, good health and environmental stability? One response is to respond directly to the quote of UMass Lowell president Moloney when she said that we were at risk of losing two million jobs in the next ten years. To make sure we keep these jobs we need to raise awareness of the programs in New England that are responding. That said, to me progressive means:

> *supporting local farming*
> *supporting disabled*
> *treating the animals better*
> *the growth of New England manufacturing*
> *apprenticeships*
> *language classes as a vehicle for inclusion and expression*

* * *

29. Directed by Kristi Jacobson and Lori Silverbush, A Place at the Table was a 2013 movie that showed the plight of childhood hunger in America.

30. Lyndsey Laton, "Lunch Lady Rises to Teacher's Union Leader and Takes on all Comers, Bluntly", The Washington Post, August 11, 2014

* * *

9. How is it that maximizing language education can make a big difference in the lives of young people while greasing the wheels of reform in other areas? There are nearly countless ways to maximize language programs without spending any more money, and so working together to do so could be a very powerful exercise. I can say this from having taught and studied languages for twenty years privately, at language schools, grammar, middle and high schools, and as part of undergraduate and graduate programs. Questions 47-85 are all about ways to maximize language program.

10. What is the meaning of the phrase "Support the Disabled, Support the Economy"? It means that supporting the disabled can be good for everyone. became clear that this phrase is the most way to think about education for the disabled. See pages 98-101 for a full range of ways to support the economy and the disabled at the same time. There are tools on those pages that can support a greater understanding of the Massachusetts economy as well.

11. What is the role of education creating critical infrastructure in New England? Three things to know about:

Credit Transfer Systems When someone enrolls in a community or state college, that credit can transfer to other schools; in Massachusetts this is through the Mass Transfer system, in New Hampshire through the NH Transfer system, and each New England state has their own version of this.

Moving Credits by Major Whereas credits might move relatively easily from institution to institution, my understanding is that credits moved by major are not always accepted so easily. You can begin research on this by checking out the Massachusetts course equivalency database link below.

See: www.mass.edu/masstransfer/equivalencies/Main.asp

The Course Equivalency Database The online "course equivalency database" allows you to search for equivalent courses within the public college system.

12. What is it important to teach personal finance and why are questions 155-157 devoted to the Salem State economics department? Young people need to understand how to manage money and that department responds to that need.

Salem State's Center for Economic Education A prime example of an institution responding to the young people's need to understand personal finance, including mortgages, financing, renting and credit is the Salem State SM.AR.T. (Save More. Act Responsibly. Thrive) program, which is a one day seminar, taught alternately by students or faculty within the SSU economics department. They seek to impart as much of the critical knowledge of managing money as they can. According to an article in *The Boston Globe*, that seminar was absolutely packed.

Personal Finance as an Elective? In the future the department may offer personal finance as an elective for both economics and non-economics majors.

Training Teachers The programs at Salem St. and Bridgewater St. also include training high school teachers on how to best teach personal finance, as well as giving them the materials to do so, thanks to the *National Council for Economic Education*.

Table 1:

Core Principles for Parents, Students and Educators to Explore

This guidebook of education is crammed with information, and the role of the tables is to review and see how the information is connected. This table reviews the main points of the first twelve questions, which are then expanded upon in the coming sections.

Core Education Points	*Vocational Education* According to MassINC., 30 to 40% of students should be in vocational programs, with as many as 50% doing a combination of the two. Are there enough seats?
	Physical Education Are students getting enough exercise to relax and focus in their work environment?
	Effective Language Learning Questions 47-85 focus on maximizing learning.
	Teaching Personal Finance High school teachers can be trained to teach this effectively, thanks to the *National Council for Economic Education.* This is the focus of pages 104-105.
Dimensions of College Credit Transfers	*Credit Transfers* Mass Transfer and NH Transfer are systems of transferring credit in NH and Mass, with each state having its own system.
	Course Equivalency Tools Course Equivalency websites allow you to see which courses are recognized by other schools.
	Transferring by Major Some departments have strict standards for transferring credit for your major, and you want to know what will and will not be recognized.
	Vocational Certificates for Credit Students can receive credit for certificates received at vocational school. See page 86 for the list of fourteen skills accepted by community and state colleges.
Aspects of Job Creation	*Community Colleges* are "a demonstrably effective way to educate and train citizens for family-sustaining jobs."
	Apprenticeships Colleges such as Vermont Tech, York County Community College and others offer apprenticeship programs.
	Manufacturing The country will need 3 million manufacturing workers in the next decade and there are training programs right here in New England. Table 15 on page 110 focuses on this.
	S.T.E.M. Coursework STEM jobs represent a large branch of jobs of the future. Pages 115-119 explores this subject in depth.
Extending Opportunities	*Supporting the Disabled, Support the Economy* See pages 98-101 for more on how the disabled can add to the economy and help create opportunities.
	Veterans and Adults The final two book sections focus on models that work for veterans, and asserts that creating effective educational models for veterans is good practice for doing so for all adults.

14

We need to do more to provide safe paths to schools for children not just for their health. You can read about existing, successful programs in New England by going to the *Safe Routes* website at saferoutespartnership.org

13-25:
Special Education and Walk-to-School Programs

"In every human being, there is a special heaven whole and unbroken."

- Paracelsus

13. What is the role of this book in supporting students in special education?
First, parents and educators can explore some highly successfully programs that might be a plus to students that have a hard time in school. Second, they can use the community college web portals on page 7 to learn about programs that are designed to lead to employment. Third, parents and educators might find new ways to answer the questions in this chapter better than I have.

- *Between 2006 and 2010, the number of Massachusetts students with serious health problems was up 59%, with the number of students with neurological disorders up 35%.* (1)

- *17 percent of Massachusetts students are in special education programs, compared with a national average of 13 percent. The rate in Massachusetts jumps to 23 percent for low-income students, who spend much of their day in separate classrooms.* (2)

14. How can giving high grades in participation in language class be helpful?
When teachers choose to base a large part of the grade on participation, they create an opportunity for students that try hard to be rewarded for it. This question is here because a language department head once asked me what percentage of the grade in Spanish class should be based on participation. He said that the average answer to that question was between 10 and 40%, although, if I remember correctly he said that he personally was a believer in 40%.

The most obvious benefit to basing a large part of the grade on participation is that students that do not test well have a chance to get good grades. However, the potential benefits go beyond that, from making students more comfortable and relaxed to engage learners in new ways. Regardless of how students or teachers feel about this, it is an interesting and important question.

* * *

1. Sheldon Berman et al., "The Rising Costs of Special Education in Massachusetts: Causes and Effects," in Rethinking Special Education for a New Century, ed.
2. Chester G. Finn, Jr., Andrew J. Rotherham, and Charles R. Hokanson, Jr. (Washington, DC: Thomas B. Fordham Foundation and Progressive Policy Institute, 2001), PDF e-book

* * *

There is no substitute for students with a great attitude that do the oral drills well and work with students that are struggling to help them do better. For that and other reasons I go into it in the section on language learning later in this chapter, I believe making the participation grade count for as much as thirty to forty percent can be a good idea, if students are truly encouraged to let all the magic inside them come out. So, we need both pieces of the puzzle; recognizing students that bring out the best in themselves and in others through classroom practice. And, giving high grades in participation can also encourage what I consider to be the best way to learn a new language, which is to read out loud.

15. What is the role of walk-to-school programs in special education? According to the national group *Safe Routes*, walking to school can help children relax and feel better in their working environment, "build a sense of neighborhood and encourage increased parental involvement at school & beyond." (3) Using the interactive map, you can read about success stories on the Safe Routes website, safe-route.org. You can also see which communities in your state offer Safe Routes programs. And, due to modern technology, you might even be able to contact and ask questions of the people in those programs.

Children struggling in school can be seen as "canaries in the coal mine", because the steps we need to take for them to adjust to the world are the same ones that the world needs. By that I mean that building the healthier, more joyful schools for struggling children will benefit all.

16. What are the causes of the growth of special education? The report *The Rising Costs of Special Education* stated; "the root causes of these increases have been factors beyond the control of the schools, such as advances in medical technology; the de-institutionalization of children with special needs, privatization of services and economic and social factors including increases in the number of children living in poverty and the number of families experiencing social and economic stress." (4) This quote is important because it shows that the source of the growth is not lax social attitudes, but rather very real environmental and biological factors.

17. How can the local economy and local employment be a plus to student learning? A vibrant local economy and local jobs can provide opportunities for learning and growth. As a Safe Routes video asserts, walking and bike paths can give children opportunities to get exercise and explore their world. (5) A robust local farming system can help provide high quality school food, green space and learning opportunities on the farm.

* * *

3. Video: Walk This Way - Safe Routes To School: Getting Children Walking, September 19, 2012, www.youtube.com/watch?v=mOeUOFSrAkA

4. Sheldon Berman et al., "The Rising Costs of Special Education in Massachusetts: Causes and Effects," in Rethinking Special Education for a New Century, ed. Chester G. Finn, Jr., Andrew J. Rotherham, and Charles R. Hokanson, Jr. (Washington, DC: Thomas B. Fordham Foundation and Progressive Policy Institute, 2001), PDF e-book, page 183.

5. Video: Walk This Way - Safe Routes To School: Getting Children Walking, September 19, 2012, www.youtube.com/watch?v

* * *

The time banking system can help create symbiotic relationships between young people, although this is an as yet relatively undeveloped system; the only such example I am aware of in New England being the *Coalition for a Better Acre* in Lowell, Massachusetts. (6)

18. What are some effects of the large size of special education? First, paying for special education often absorbs a great deal of the school budget, which arguably can indirectly lead to larger classroom size and therefore less personalized attention for the average student. (7) In Massachusetts, 50% of the Education budget is spent on the 17% of students in special education. (8)

Second, teachers often have to modify teaching style to accommodate these students, such as putting certain students in the first row, which isn't a big deal unless there are ten other students in the class that also need special attention. So, there are plenty of ideas to explore in special education outside the classroom; now let's look at some ideas inside the classroom.

19. Why are community colleges of critical importance to children in special education? Community colleges offer affordable programs locally. Specifically, many community colleges are responding to the need for skilled workers in manufacturing programs, through industry partnerships and other practical programs. Community colleges are also affordable and credits earned there can be easily transferred with the new credit transfer systems. This means families can take a chance on community college programs with less financial risk and potentially large rewards.

20. How might vocational education help students struggling in the traditional classroom? Many are better off learning hands on, marketable skills. As you may know by now, in Massachusetts, only seven percent of students are in vocational programs, although in the opinion of *MassINC.*, thirty to forty percent of students would be better off in vocational studies, while as many as fifty percent should be doing a combination of vocational and traditional studies. (9) "Comprehensive" high schools, or those that have traditional and vocational programs on one campus may have an advantage, because doing a combination of traditional and vocational studies is more feasible.

It should also be noted that the support systems for vocational studies have increased the value of the choice to pursue vocational studies. One aspect of this support are the various articulation agreements, which mean that students can often get credit at community colleges with a certificate received at a vocational school. (see question 23) And, the value of these certificates received at community colleges is high, because the coursework at some of these colleges is increasingly geared toward employment.

* * *

6. Coalition for a Better Acre, Building and Strengthening our Communities. www.cbacre.org/
7. Sheldon Berman et al.
8. Ibid
9. The State of the American Dream MassINC (1996)

* * *

18

21. How can art and expressive programs be good for special education?
Two years in special education working with those with extreme emotional and neurological disorders taught me the power of daily art class. In a school day that can feel long and stressful, there's nothing like one period during which everyone is happy. Students acquired skill sets that are compounded during the course of the years in school and I witnessed junior and seniors doing amazing work. So, how will we find the time and money for this?

22. How can maximizing language programs make a big difference to students in special education? The reality is that innovation is hard for teachers with all the pressures and potential issues from parents, students, and the school administration. But, reading out loud can boost student learning greatly. See questions 45-87, as they focus strictly on maximizing language programs.

23. How can schools provide pathways to jobs for students that have had a hard time with book learning? The good news is many colleges in New England have begun to adapt to all kinds of students. In the course of working in special education, I witnessed tragic situations in which young people had little hope. I remember one high school where about half of the graduating students were not going to college after school. That's not necessarily a bad thing, but most also had no job or any idea where to get one. New steps to reach those young people include;

The Articulation Agreements The value of the 2011 Articulation Agreements is they recognize achievement at vocational schools by granting college credit for certificates received. With the introduction of the agreements in 2011, students can now continue their vocational education at community colleges. (10)

Apprenticeship Programs Schools like Vermont Technical College and York County Community College in Maine match students with mentors in electrical work and plumbing while supporting the relationship with classroom time. Apart from these apprenticeship models, there are others to learn about on page 89.

MEP Trainings The trainings are seven to eight weeks long, or 280 hours, which are sponsored by the six Manufacturing Extension Partnerships in the six New England states prepare students for basic manufacturing work. After completing the workshops, workers are proficient in CNC, or Computer Numerical Control.

Coursework in Advanced Manufacturing UNH, The University of Maine and others now offer highly effective training for students that want to go into manufacturing. Table 15 on page 110 has more information on that.

Vocational education no longer is just limited to carpentry, plumbing, mechanics, electronics and beauty school. Today, they offer a chance for a good salary with a fraction of the student debt.

* * *

10. The Massachusetts Community Colleges Executive Office (MCCEO) and the State Universities Council of Presidents joined together to answer a call from the Department of Higher Education's Task Force on Collaboration and Efficiency. The councils are comprised of twenty-four PACE (Partnership to Advance Collaboration & Efficiency) charter members (fifteen community colleges and 9 state universities) who oversee the Articulation Agreements for the state.
* * *

Average Salaries Per Year from Vocational Education

Job	Entry Level
Network Administration	$64,820.00
Cyber Security	$85,404.00
Drafter	$52,000.00
Web Design	$61,805.00
Manufacturing Engineer	$71,000.00
Office Worker	$44,000.00
Graphic Design	$54,392.00

See: The full list of occupations and salary growth expectations at Salary.com

High Costs in Boston According to Jumpshell.com, if he/she lives alone a Boston renter's average cost per year including food and utilities is $26,000 (Food $4,200, Rent $20,400, Utilities $900). Then Bostonrealestate.com says you need to earn $92,796.90 to afford the mortgage on a home with the median price of $449,000, according to HSH findings. The average monthly payment – assuming a 20 percent down payment and an interest rate of 4.03 percent for a 30-year, fixed rate mortgage – would be between $2,165.26 monthly and $25,983.12 a year. This is a goal that is easier to reach with a vocational education without high college debt.

Apprenticeships in and North of Boston In Wells, Maine, about two hours north of Boston, York County Community College offers both plumbing and apprentice-ship programs by which workers in the trades can be matched with a tradesman to act as a mentor while they can continue their education at the college level. (11) These kinds of apprenticeships seems to be making their way further south, though; see question 99 on page 56 for some efforts within the city of Boston.

The coursework offered in advanced manufacturing at Vermont, New Hampshire and Maine community colleges is long overdue; manufacturers have been crying out for skilled workers for decades.

* * *

11. The first two colleges in New England with apprenticeships programs that I learned about are York County Community College (Maine) and Vermont Technical College. I use these two as examples as I have had the opportunity to interview representatives from both schools.
www.vtc.edu/academics/continuing-education-workforce-development/programs/electrical-and-plumbing/apprenticeship
York County Community College, "Pratt and Whitney Employees Complete Apprenticeship Program", May 26, 2017. www.yccc.edu/press_release/pratt-whitney-employees-complete-apprentice-ship-program-2/

* * *

Comprehensive Support of the Trades

The introduction of the Articulation Agreements, apprenticeship programs and training in manufacturing may be one reason why community college enrollment in Maine has risen from 10,000 to 18,000 in ten years. Perhaps this kind of programming in all six New England states will create one dimension of the infrastructure that can reach some of the lost boys and girls in the region. (12)

24. What is "tracking" and how is it relevant to Special Education? According to the critics, "Tracking," is the practice of putting students in low or high level classes has three main problems. The first is that there is often very little mobility, meaning that students can be stuck there for their whole school career. The second problem is the stigmatization that comes with being in the lower track, which can be tough to deal with emotionally. The third issue is the tendency for struggling students to be taught methods "dominated by strategies that are passive; students do lots of worksheets, they tend to work alone."(13) According to recent articles on tracking, students need rich content, group problem-solving activities and interaction with their peers.

For those looking for one good article on tracking, see Anne Wheelock's article in the October 1992 publication of *Educational Leadership* titled "The Case for Untracking."(14) In that article, she discusses "dismantling unproductive grouping practices that have undermined education for all but a few students." She goes on to emphasize a number of key principles, including "A Belief that All Students can Learn" and "A Belief in Change as a Process." A second article on tracking is "On Restructuring Schools: A Conversation with Al Shanker; Making the Best of Schools."(15) As for Al Shanker, his story is an interesting one; he was not only the President of the American Federation of Teachers but is also credited with being the originator of the idea of charter schools.

25. What is one model for preparing young people with physical and/or mental health issues for the work force? One innovative way was to employ young, disabled people at a coffee shop (16) which was one of many examples promoted by the *Institute for Community Inclusion*. (17)

* * *

12. Massachusetts Community Colleges. "Partnerships".
www.masscc.org/partnerships-initiatives/partnerships
13. John O'Neil "On Tracking and Individual Differences: A Conversation with Jeannie Oakes" October 1992. www.ascd.org/
14. Anne Wheelock, "The Case for Untracking", Association for Supervision and Curriculum Development, October1992. www.ascd.org/
15. Albert Shanker, United Federation of Teachers, "Who We Are".
www.uft.org/who-we-are/history/albert-shanker
16. New Cafe Breaks Ground in Peabody, in More Ways than One". *The Salem News*. 11/27,/2016
17. The Institute for Community Inclusion. Let's Get Started on Your Plan! The Institute for Community Inclusion is a group that aims to integrate the disabled into mainstream life. One of their tools is on the "Future Planning Page". Among many other resources of The ICI is by Helen Liedtke, an Allen C. Crocker Fellow 2015/2016, "Creating Inclusive Play and Community Spaces; An Out of the Box Approach to social and community inclusion.

* * *

Support the Disabled, Support the Economy

In 2015-2016, when this book was originally written, this chapter explored creating employment. It was asked: "How many of those new jobs, if we work together to create them, could go to the disabled?" About 28,000 people in Massachusetts work in agriculture, and I believe that we might get that number to 38,000 and beyond if we work together. However, the question should be; "How many of those jobs could go to the disabled?" For example, some of those jobs must involve the sorting of produce that someone with no use of their legs could do? The table on page 101 focuses on ways to support the disabled.

Job Variety Locally

Another dimension of creating employment is to create jobs that are suited to different temperaments. And, if we can create these jobs locally, whereby employees don't need to spend the money and energy commuting, all the better. To that end, two models that can help with this are The People's Academy and the Boston Public Market.

The People's Academy The *"mission is to provide opportunities for training and mentoring to men, women and at risk youth in the inner city, making them employable"*. This model is worthy of study, as it involves using a relatively small amount of money to pass on a highly valuable skill. Their current goal is to graduate thirty students a year.

See: www.peoplesacademyinc.org/

Boston Public Market With local stores going out of business due to internet competition or other factors, the approach of the BPM is pure gold; thrit-five vendors split rent and overhead costs in one shared space. What this means is that small local businesses can sell their products, which could in turn create jobs for struggling youth, if only they had some guidance and opportunity. It also could be particularly supportive of job creation at small New England farms.

See: www.bostonpublicmarket.org/

If we put our heads together on the themes of this question, we should be able to offer more opportunities to young people. The Boston Public market model may also represent a way to offer opportunities to small businesses.

Why was physical education important then and not today? What has changed?

26-38:
Physical Education as a Tool for Health and Better Focus in the Classroom

"Taking time from physical education does not result in more learning in other areas." - Guy Le Masurier and Charles B. Corbin

26. What have I witnessed with regards to physical education during my time working in the schools? In my experience teaching, they're not a priority. After working for seven years in grammar and high schools, including two years in special education, I noticed that few of the behavioral problems and attention difficulties students faced were addressed with physical activity. I wondered if maybe the reason was the focus on team sports; which are a great outlet for some, but not all. Perhaps with the pressures of testing and budget constraints, physical education programs get put on the back burner.

The Exception: the Ski Academy With exception of very unique physical programs I witnessed while working at a ski academy in New Hampshire, where the students seemed happy, I never worked at a school that made daily physical activity a priority.

27. How important is recess to the health of children? Just as I believe Charles B. Corbin that *"taking time from physical education does not result in more learning in other areas,"* I believe cutting recess is a bad idea. In fifteen years teaching, including a few years with students with extreme emotional and neurological disorders, I saw recess helped students relax and focus. So, as opposed to cutting back recess to use extra time to prepare students for tests, it may be that *they need more time to play.*

"On Recess" in The Brookline Tab An excellent article that points out the value of recess with excellent documentation was titled "Commentary: Brookline Should Take the Lead on Maximum Recess", by Dr. Rebecca G. Breslow, published on November 10, 2017. One reason I liked the article is because both the main points of contention *and the main takeaways* are relevant to any community. The following quote summarizes much of the article;

"Recess can help to refocus children, stimulating them to perform at a higher cognitive level when they return to academic activities. It affords them time to engage their peers in an unstructured way and learn how to successfully negotiate different social situations. It provides an outlet for stress release against the rigors of a full and demanding school day".

The article is packed with great information and sources that parents might discuss with each other. Who knows, ambitious journalists may see some value in the article when writing about the contentious issue in the community they serve.

28. Are there any good models of physical education that other physical education teachers might learn from? I really liked a series of three videos I saw on youtube, each of which profiled games that work really well, depending on the amount of space available. And, not only do the teachers explain the game before the class demonstrated it, they explained what items were needed to play the game, such as cones, balls, nets or whatever else.

Phys. Ed. Tutorial Small Space Games In this video the games Rock/Paper/Scissors, Kaboom Ball, and Ga Ga (with or without the Human Wall) were explained.

Phys. Ed. Tutorial Mid Sized Space Games Plunger, Duck Hunt and Paintball (with balls not paint guns) were demonstrated.

Phys. Ed. Tutorial Large Spaces Games Indiana Jones, 4 Corner Omnikin, Chaos, Opposites and Mat Madness were demonstrated in a large gymnasium. (1)

This kind of inclusion can help prevent bullying. Although there still is plenty of aggressive, direct bullying, the modern version often involves complicated psychological attacks by multiple people on one student.

29. What is one way to find the time for physical education? One answer is for students to be able to do physical education instead of study hall. Having served as a proctor for many study halls, it pained me to be so strict with students when I knew that some of them just really needed to take a break from academics and get some exercise. It just seemed totally unrealistic and unfair to have to reprimand students who couldn't sit perfectly still with book learning all day – don't they deserve to run around and have some fun once in a while?

30. What is one quote on the state of physical education programs? According to the Centers for Disease Control, *"Nearly half — 46 percent — of high school students were not attending any P.E. classes when surveyed by the Centers for Disease Control; still others have P.E. for only one-third of the year."* (2) I had no trouble believing this statistic after difficult experiences with agitated students in study halls.

The Role of Guidance Counselors When talking about how more or better physical education might help students, it seems appropriate to also look at the role of guidance counseling. As was stated in an interview on WBUR; *"according to the Association for College Admission Counseling, the average American school now has one guidance counselor for every 500 students".* As Bill Symonds, the director of the Global Pathways Institute said; "I think it's really the black hole in the American education system". So, as we look to correct deficiencies in physical education, we might also be aware of a second deficiency that also impacts student health.

* * *

1. In 2017 the Massachusetts Lieutenant Governor initiated a push to create laws on the possession and distribution of images and videos of other people. This is relevant to physical education, as showering is often involved after sports or recess. Massachusetts General Laws Chapter 272, Sections 105 and 99 governs this subject, for both adults and minors on possession and distribution.

2. Centers for Disease Control. "Healthy Youth and Physical Activity." www.cdc.gov/healthyyouth/physicalactivity/facts.htm

* * *

31. What is a good place for parents or educators to start to learn about *Safe Routes* programs? A good place to start might be the *Safe Routes Interactive Map*, in order to see the different case studies for different communities, and how each adjusted to the challenges. Some of the places the programs are located are rural, whereas some are urban. Some might have very few walking paths.

There are two case studies I think of as my "favorites", but I'll let readers do their own research to see which programs they like or learn from the most.

32. Why is physical education so valuable and why might it regain its prominence as a valuable profession? For starters, I think people will recognize that it's not a distraction, but rather a critical dimension of education. In the article "Top 10 Reasons for Quality Physical Education", Guy Le Masurier and Charles B. Corbin articulate the core principle, when they said; "*Taking time from physical education does not result in more learning in other areas.*" (3) However, my favorite quote is from the historian Roberta Park, who noted that;

"*During the 20th century, medicine emerged as the renaissance profession because of the development of a sound scientific base.*" (4) She went on to say that the physical education teacher "*has become the renaissance profession of the new millennium*" (5) After all, who is in a greater position to contribute to the health of children than the teacher that supervises their daily exercise? The truth is that with so many different ages and issues to deal with, the job can be tricky. Myra and David Sadker wrote the following comment on one demographic;

"*Confident about their physical abilities and other talents in earlier years, girls of ages 10 through 13 experience a psychological reversal in their development. Cultural messages and societal pressures substantially affect their development and drive them into a downward psychological tailspin.*" (6)

Clearly, any teacher that was able to use their knowledge and skills to help this or any other demographic feel better should be a prized asset indeed, and perhaps it's just a matter of time until more people see that.

* * *

3. This statistic was quoted on a March 2014 Edition of Beat the Press, a PBS roundtable style show hosted by Emily Rooney
4. Guy Le Masurier and Charles B. Corbin, "Top Ten Reasons for Quality Physical Education," www.aahperd.org/naspe/publications/teachingtools/upload/top10reasonsforqualitype.pdf, May14, 2013
5. Corbin and Le Masurier
6. Linda A. Catelli, "Failing at Fairness: How America's Schools Cheat Girls".

* * *

33. Might physical education and language learning be combined to make language learning more accessible? I hope so. In the American high schools I taught at, the culture was to sit still and do rote learning, with way too much grammar at an early phase. It is this experience that led me to ask if "kinetic language learning" might be a good fit for some students and maybe even be more relaxed for the next class.

The class format could be simple; a rotation between four minutes of exercise, followed by four minutes of listening or reading out loud, for one classroom period. Eight four minute rounds with one minute of rest comes to forty minutes. The ideal outcome would be that everyone gets a little exercise and practices their Spanish, including reading out loud, with authentic emotion. If the written work were done as part of homework at night, and this class was done right, it could lead to breakout results. I think great teachers with good relations with parents and the administration could make it happen. It probably is happening already.

34. Are the walk-to-school programs advocated in this book a substitute for physical education? No, but they might be part of the whole picture of creating health in children. The programs sponsored by *Safe Routes* help students find walking routes to school, but I would hope that they don't preclude the perceived need for physical education. By utilizing the *Safe Routes* interactive map you can click on a state and read about existing programs near you. The *Safe Routes* programs also create employment opportunities, as these programs need coordinators at a local, regional and national level. Although much of the work is done by parent or community volunteers, they need people to help out with implementation.

35. Are there any good examples of university coursework that meets the physical needs of students or college employees? The "Wildcat Workout Project" at the University of New Hampshire is an example of a university committing to the health of employees. "UNH Employees (and dependents 18 and older) can take advantage of group fitness classes led by coaches and fitness professionals from UNH Athletics. This pilot program is a series of 45-60 minute classes that will raise your heart rate, make you sweat, and still get you back to your desk on time." (7)

36. Are there any existing, successful examples of healthy good school food? To get the full benefits of exercise or walking to school, children need to eat well. The French movie Les Enfants Nous Accuseront was one response, and it profiled one school that grew and ate its own food. (8)

As the young Brit Jamie Oliver put it; *"This food revolution is about saving American's health by changing the way they eat…if you care about your kids and their future, take this revolution and make it your own."* (9)

* * *

7. "Wildcat Workout Project", Healthy UNH. www.unh.edu/healthyunh/wildcat-workout-project

8. Les Enfants Nous Accuseront: 2008. 1 Hour, 52 Minuites. English Title: Food Beware: The French Organic Revolution. IMDB

9. Jamie Oliver's Food Revolution www.jamieoliver.com/us/foundation/jamies-food-revolution/about_jamie_oliver

* * *

Childhood Hunger You might think serious childhood hunger is rare in the United States, but according to the movie *A Place at the Table* it's quite common. The movie shares that part of the problem is a pre-conceived notion of what hungry looks like. Some of the children going hungry might have a healthy weight but they're getting very little nutrition, which can mean the children look normal but don't feel good enough to focus at school.

Hunger at Public Colleges A survey of administrators at the 29 state colleges and universities in Massachusetts shows that 24 operate food pantries on campus or work with community food banks, and say that 38% of administrators report seeing the number of students living with "food insecurity" grow. Food insecurity is roughly defined as a lack of consistent access to food. Food pantries also witnessed a 34% rise in students utilizing their services. Massachusetts Colleges are stepping up to remedy this dilemma.

I make mention of the issue of hunger in the context of physical education for obvious reasons, and I'm sure most readers get that.

37. Beyond *Safe Routes*, are there any models of walk-to-school programs that support communities? Yes, the national group *Safe Routes* has had successes in virtually every state, (10) but every community concerned with making their city the nicest place it can be should learn about the Pedestrian, Bike and Information Center (PBIC). The PBIC also offers coursework (with a PDF outline for future teachers) that educates people on the complicated aspects of creating a city friendly to walkers and bikers. The only issue is that not many colleges offer the curriculum. (11) You can see the list of schools that do offer the courses in question 115. (12)

38. Do I have any experience with gym classes that were run especially well? Yes, some years ago I worked in special education, as I went with the students to gym class. I had the pleasure of watching a gym teacher that had been teaching for thirty-five years teach highly structured classes in which all the children had the time of their lives, including one student that we were all worried about. It's a simple story but it's important; true professionals can give children the fun and well-being they need to have a great day, and you really can't put a price on that.

* * *

10. Michael Levenson, "State's Public Colleges See Rise in Hunger, Homelessness, The Boston Globe, January 25, 2017, See also: WBUR, Boston University Radio, "Mass. Public Campuses See More Hungry And Homeless Students". www.wbur.org/

11. Pedestrian, Bike and Information Center. "Maps".
www.maps.saferoutesinfo.org

12. PBIC, or Pedestrian Bike and Information Center.

* * *

Vocational Schools have a lot more to offer than they used to in the past. Some vocational trades pay almost $100,000 a year today.

39-46:

Adult Education and Adjunct Professors

"Modern manufacturing has had a profound impact on both our country and our economy. I cannot think of a more appropriate year to truly celebrate this than 2016, as we are in the midst right now of another manufacturing renaissance, right here at home."

– Barbara Finkelstein, President of York County Community College

39. How can we maximize education in New England for adults while securing a better future for adjuncts? Adding value to the community college system can be a vehicle for New Englanders to reach their goals while simutaneously helping to secure a bright future for New England adjuncts.

40. What were the main areas of adult education and how has that changed? Ten years ago, remedial education, English and special interest subjects were core areas of study. English language courses were designed to help recent arrivals get working skills in English. (1) However, new programs at community colleges have changed adult education, and now offer apprenticeships, industry partnerships, recognition of prior learning credits and much, much more.

York County Community College in Wells, Maine offers innovative apprenticeship programs in plumbing and electrical, with similar programs at Vermont Technical College. These and other programs can work for older students as well. Page 89 has a list of some of these apprenticeships.

41. How serious is the need for better English language instruction? Workers and employers benefit if instruction of English is more effective. The report entitled "New Skills for the New Economy," by MassINC., stated that in Massachusetts, 150,000 workers speak little or no English, and it limits their opportunities. (2)

42. How can we help workers acquire English language skills? Choosing the best possible books can help a great deal. In my experience, the best models for those books are the ones used by the language schools such as The *Berlitz School* or *Inlingua*. When I taught there, the books easy to use and students all made consistent progress. The use of frequency dictionaries can help although that is the focus of question 77 on page 43. However, most important is the proper support for teachers and whatever method they choose.

* * *

1. New Skills for the New Economy, by MassINC. The 1996 MassINC. report The State of the American Dream in New England, which fell into my hands in 1997, greatly influenced my writing on education. That influence is still strong here. A new report by Andy Sum et al., The State of the American Dream in Massachusetts, was released in 2002 (Boston: MassINC, 2002),. www.massinc. org/Research/The-State-of-the-American-Dream.aspx.

2. Ibid.

* * *

43. How do we support quality of life for New England adjuncts? Any and every way we can. A good start is through learning to maximize and protect Social Security for our adjuncts, many of whom struggle and suffer a great deal. One Social Security Course model is profiled on page 135, question 206. With 82 different pathways to enrollment in Social Security, the University of Texas course is a model for helping folks choose the right pathway. In the meantime, adjuncts can assure their benefits are safe with the Social Security Trust Fund Tracker.

See: ssa.gov/policy/social-security-long-term-financial-outlook.html

44. How might more discussion of trade deals on campus lead to revenue that might result in a better deal for adjuncts? The best possible trade deals will lead to the best possible sales opportunities for New England manufacturers, farmers and businesses, the increase in tax revenue that could be used to fund the massive deferred maintenance at New England public colleges. It will feel great when we have an awesome trade deal with our awesome friends in Mexico. Perhaps healthy discussions on campus can lead to this relationship. (3) The other contribution we need is for professors to be a part of these conversations on trade deals, or economists and environmentalists weighing in their respective fields on TV.

45. How can a boost in apprenticeships, industry partnerships and manufacturing lead to opportunities for adjunct professors? Ideally, an increase in practical employment will lead to more choosing to attend coursework at community colleges, which will in turn lead to a greater need for professors that teach subjects such as English, Math or Literature.

46. How and why can we help struggling adjunct professors? Helping out adjunct professors is good for adjuncts, students and the colleges and universities they work at. Adjunct problems are particularly relevant to Boston because of the huge number of colleges and high housing costs. However, if we can figure out some solutions, we can help them and be a model for other communities in New England. Some sad quotes about the situation:

"Adjuncts have large teaching loads, are poorly paid, often have to share cramped office space and get no health insurance." Los Angeles Times (4)

"with a lack of access to personal office space, computers, library resources, and curriculum guidelines, among other things, the education experience of students suffers, both inside and outside of the classroom."

The Chronicle for Higher Education *(5)*

* * *

3. "President Trump Announces New Trade Deal with Mexico", Fox News, August 27, 2018. "Joined on the phone by President Nieto, President Trump announces the United States-Mexico Trade Agreement, and understanding with Mexico that could lead to overhaul of NAFTA."
4. Charlotte Allen, "The highly educated, badly paid, often abused adjunct professors", Los Angeles Times, December 22, 2013. www.latimes.com/opinion/
5. Goldstene, Claire, "The Politics of Contingent Academic Labor," National Education Association. www.nea.org/home/53403.htm

* * *

8 Challenges Related to Supporting Adjuncts Healthy

There are other harsh realities that affect New England adjuncts, including declining enrollment in colleges nationwide, (6) the fact that so much learning has gone online. This is compounded by the fact that there are so many colleges in New England; over one hundred in Massachusetts and over two hundred in New England.

1. Declining Enrollment (Byrne. Wicked Local Danvers)
2. Decreasing Revenues. (Vedder. Forbes)
3. Colleges Closing Doors. (America's Lost Colleges)
4. Retention Rates. Many enroll in community
   colleges, but retention rates tell the full story.
(www.mass.edu)
5. Smaller Applicant Pool. (Vedder)
6. Many say they would rather work and make money. (Byrne)
7. Many college graduates struggle to find work.
(Weber, Korn)
8. Rising Annual Federal Interest Payments (7)

Staying Relevant: 8 Existing Successes

As I see it, the only answer to all of the issues above is to evolve and become as relevant as possible. Each and every question in this book is posed that we might then find answers to this, but below are my favorite responses.

1. Living and Learning Houses L&L Houses represent a new frontier of opportunity to add value to time spent on campus. The value that adjuncts might add to student learning as leaders of these houses while saving money is exciting!

2. Teach Personal Finance Personal finance programs of the caliber of the Salem State Economics department adds value to the entire college experience.

3. STEM The article by Steve Lohr was a gamechanger. Educating students and educators about the realities of STEM is key to success of modern colleges. See pages 115-119 for more.

4. Address Weak Points in Green Plans Campus "Green Plans" boost relevance of campus work. This should include the "Big Three" weak points: conservation, animal cruelty and species extinction.

5. The Fred Berry Standard: Support the Disabled, Support the Economy, as outlined on pages 98-101, is an exercise in supporting the Massachusetts economy.

6. Manufacturing The successes of manufacturing centers at the University of New Hampshire and University of Maine is something to be built upon.

7. Apprenticeships These are a key part of future job creation. See page 89 for examples.

8. Serve Veterans Attracting veterans back to campus is all about becoming relevant: doing so means building an effective adult education system.

* * *

6. Colleen Flaherty "A Push to Plan for Adjuncts and Equity". June 22, 2021 *Inside Higher Ed.*
7. Congressional Budget Office: Federal Net Interest Costs: A Primer.
* * *

Table 2:
Building Quality of Life for Adjuncts

Fighting for adjunct professors is about fighting for an overworked, underpaid group that makes up 74% of teaching staff. As Maria Maisto, President of the New Faculty Majority said; "Faculty working conditions are student learning conditions, but we realize that people don't get that connection." For the sources article, see: "How Universities Treat Adjuncts Limits Their Effectiveness in the Classroom, Report Says, by Audrey Williams June, in The Chronicle of Higher Education on August 23, 2012.

Staying Relevant	With over two hundred colleges in New England and enrollment declining nationally, colleges need to adapt to maintain staffing. Question 103 on page reflects on the closure of Green Mountain College in Vermont, which brought heartache to students. faculty and devoted alumni.
Union Options	1."Unionization really is the best option for adjunct professors." Dante Ramos "Adjunct Professor Unionize, Revealing Deeper Malaise", The Boston Globe, March 24, 2016. 2. *National Unions:* Service Employees International Union, the American Federation of Teachers and the National Education Association. 3. *State Unions* include the Community College Association. 4. *College Unions* specific to each college.
Adjunct Mutual Support	1. *The New Faculty Majority* is a leader in exploring affordable health care and health care models for adjuncts. 2. Time banks can be a excellent support system for adjunct professors. Question 131 explores this. **See:** www.HourWorld.org 3. The CSA at UMass Stockbridge that sells healthy, affordable food to community members is a good model for keeping folks happy and fed. 4. Adjuncts can assure their benefits are safe with the Social Security Trust Fund Tracker below. ssa.gov/policy/social-security-long-term-financial-outlook.html
Housing Successes	1. *Project Ground Floor* Co-ownership of housing can help adjuncts lower bills and build capital. Learn about *Project Ground Floor* in question 76. 2. Living and Learning houses offer on campus housing for leadership work. Question 84 tells of the Reed College "visiting scholars" model.

47-86
Maximizing Language Programs

Whereas every other section of this book required extensive research, this section is a little different, as I've been teaching and studying languages since 1995. What that means is I have some knowledge. The potential positive effect of language programs, beyond the obvious practical benefits of skill acquisition, are important. As different parts of the world connect, effective communication and expression will be key.

47. Do better language programs need to cost more? No, although a good supply of easy readers or new software can be expensive. In fact , making the class goal specific is half the battle. My most radical belief is that any school that wants outstanding language programs can have them, if only they go about it that way. That said, this is a a very in depth chapter, with thirty questions featuring some succesful ideas and models. Some of the chapter themes are:

> *the role of oral drills*
> *theories on the participation grade*
> *language exchange sites*
> *easy readers*
> *the role of language exchanges*
> *needs of English language learners*

48. What is the role of oral drills? Oral drills bring the language alive. Although, as teachers at the middle and high school level know, the drills need to be very specific. Easy reading and oral drills can give students the practice they need to make progress every day. And, if you make progress every day, you don't have to worry. One way to encourage effective drills is to base a large part of the grade on participation. I met one language teacher that based 40% of the grade on this, which can be good both for learning and promoting a positive classroom culture. It is also supportive of students that try that may not test well.

49. How can better language programs be good for cooperation and job creation? As much as the English language continues to spread throughout the world, so too does the value that people place on those that speak the native tongue of any given country. Though English has become increasingly widespread, we're already seeing an increasing insistence on maintenance of the native language and culture. (1) For example, more Germans learning Polish and Poles learning German, as opposed to the two groups strictly learning English. However, here in the United States, the need for more effective language learning is pragmatic; students who are learning English drop out of school more.

* * *

1. Sally Weale, "Britons Should learn Polish, Punjabi and Urdu to boost social cohesion". January 18, 2017. *The Guardian.*

* * *

50. How can language exchange sites contribute to student learning? Boys and girls doing language exchanges and eventually even talk about ways to make the world a better place. For many parents whose children study Spanish in school, better job opportunities or more rewarding vacations in South America may seem like the biggest benefits. However, these exchanges are just one part of the steps forward that can help to make language learning in the schools much more effective. Three of the free online sites for young people to do exchanges are WeSpeke, Speaky and HiNative. There are other language exchange sites where you can pay for a tutor, but these are some of the free sites.

Collaboration Across Borders One way for language learners to connect is to do online exchanges. Another way for these exchanges to happen is classroom-to-classroom. I know of one Italian department doing exchanges with a class in Italy, although I'm sure that there are many other examples.

Sticking up for Mother Nature The People's Climate Summit decided to amend the Ecuadorian constitution to include "equal rights to Mother Nature", for the continent has lashed back at the abusive behavior of foreign corporations on many fronts. (2) This is good news, in part because it sets the stage for language programs that lead to productive communication between the younger generations in the Americas.

51. What are a few main aspects of quality K-12 language courses? Three areas are; easy readers, oral drills, and a correct application of the participation grade.

Easy Readers Reading in the target language gives students the massive repetition of vocabulary and grammar they need. There are many easy readers out there, but I personally prefer the ones that state the number of words the book utilizes. For example, *Pobre Ana* by Blaine Ray is a "300", meaning that the books uses only the 300 highest frequency words. However, reading the book once isn't enough; it can be read dozens of times in different ways while the teacher asks a variety of comprehension questions.

Oral Drills Oral drills can bring the language alive in the classroom, but teachers need to be sure to make them specific. Also, the culture of how to do oral drills in language class is something that needs to be learned in the younger grades, because keeping the drills focused can be a challenge.

The Participation Grade This can change the classroom culture in many positive ways, although there is some disagreement as to what percentage of the final grade should be based on participation. Some say as little as 10%, but I have known teachers that base as much as 40% of the final grade on this.

The Confession I should say that during fifteen years I taught languages, I never perfected the balance of these four key dimensions of language study. When I worked in language schools in Europe it was easier, because the students were highly motivated adults, and those schools (Berlitz and Inlingua) provided excellent books. So, success was easy. I hope more American students will get to experience this kind of success.

* * *

2. People's Climate Summit Celsias, "South America Leading the Push toward Sustainability," Clean Techies, May 5, 2010

* * *

52. How can "language houses" lead to greater language learning, as well as add value to the overall college experience? Called "Living and Learning" houses at some schools, language houses are a great way for students studying the same language at a college to work together and help each other reach their goals. In my experience, though, most colleges have only begun to take advantage of the opportunities that a language house on campus can provide.

Good Neighbors in the Americas The thing is, my experiences with college language houses date back to the 1990's when I was an undergraduate. However, a lot has changed since then As Miguel Tinker-Salas, a professor of Latin American history at Pomona College in Claremont, Calif. says;

"The last 10 years have produced dramatic changes in Latin America…it's no longer the backyard where, either through benign neglect or direct intervention, the US could more or less freely act to achieve its goals."

In other words, American investments south of the border are no longer the only game in town, and Americans that wish to explore opportunities elsewhere in the Americas are going to have to learn some cultural appreciation. (3)

53. How can college language houses build better relationships? Speaking strictly for me, I have seen few things nicer than young people working to-gether to learn each other's language. And it seems to me that not only might these language houses facilitates more of these relationships between students living in the house, in some cases they might choose to extend certain oppor-tunities to the community. Building symbiotic relationships between people and communities in the Americas is going to require better communication, and effective study of Spanish, Portuguese, and language houses can help.

The Tandem Plus Model The section on languages at the universities promotes the idea of language exchanges via computer, as done by the Tandem Plus Pro-gram at the University of Minnesota, (4) and this is certainly something that could be done as part of the language house experience.

Program Houses Within New England, there are plenty of examples of col-lege language houses, and analyses of how different program houses promote student learning could be the subject of an entire book. In the meantime, you can see "Four New Program Houses Approved for Next Year", written by Jake Lahut of *The Wesleyan Argus* for examples. Each of those houses represent models that other schools might learn from.

* * *

3. Lafranche, Howard "US No Longer Towers Over Latin America", Christian Science Monitor. April 18, 2009
4. Tandem Plus", Pomona College of Liberal Arts Language Center, University of Minnesota,
* * *

54. How can effective English as a Second Language Programs facilitate smoother integration of recent adult immigrants? According to the *MassINC.* publication *New Skills for the New Economy*, better English skills is one of the most needed changes in the Massachusetts workforce. (5) More effective English language programs means recent immigrants integrated more effectively. *"Students who are learning English drop out of school more and graduate less regularly than any other group. Their test scores are far off the state average -- between 50 and 84 percent scored "warning/failing" on last year's MCAS test, depending on the subject -- and there's little evidence that they're catching up."*

- Mass DOE, School and District Profiles

55. How can government agencies benefit from Americans learning foreign languages? Government agencies are always looking for speakers of other languages. (6) Additionally, under new laws many hospitals need to have bilingual staff to speak with patients. Hospitals have difficulty with this, and it is an added cost. According to Richard Brecht,

"The U.S. education system...simply has not made the investment in language required to provide the government with an adequate pool of linguistic expertise from which to recruit to meet its needs." (7)

Mr. Brecht certainly has a point, which is one more reason for school and college language departments to look at existing, successful models of other departments. This process can be facilitated by the existence of "course equivalency websites", by which course credits can be exchanged, which will naturally lead to new communication. For one example of such a credit transfer page, see the page "Undergraduate Credit Transfer" on the page of The Registrar of the University of Vermont.

See: www.uvm.edu/registrar/undergraduate-transfer-credit

56. What is the role of language programs in connecting communities? Language programs are one means for creating connections between communities and they can be a tool to give voice to other world cultures. Students in North and South America learning each others language might learn about conservation projects. Costa Rica, with 25% of its land under national protection, is a model for the hemisphere. Chile recently set aside 11 million acres for a national park; these are possible clasroom topics.

I happen to know that one Italian class that does classroom-to-classroom teaching, by which a class of students in Italy learning English and students at learning Italian connect through a classroom monitor. This opens up endless new possibilities.

* * *

5. MassINC. "New Skills for the New Economy", 2002

6. Centers for Languages, Literatures and Cultures, Ohio State University. cllc.osu.edu/undergraduate/careers/broad-spectrum/government

7. Richard Brecht, "The Language Crisis in the War on Terror," The Eisenhower Institute, Gettysburg College, October 24, 2002, www.eisenhowerinstitute.org/

* * *

57. Is there new technology to utilize in language instruction? The "Tandem Plus" programs at the University of Minnesota, where students engage in virtual language exchanges through Skype (8) is a low cost approach to giving students the practice that they need. I know how effective Skype is for language lessons because I used to get lessons in Chinese this way, and sharing the screen with the teacher meant the teacher could read while I did my best to follow along. This method works well for languages that are hard to read or pronounce.

58. How does instruction at language schools differ from high schools? After teaching English at the *Berlitz* and *Inlingua* language schools in Bonn, Germany, I decided to teach high school Spanish. What I found was a vast contrast between the teaching styles at the language schools and those of the high schools. Whereas virtually all students at my language school were progressing visibly from week to week, at the high school the students were putting in a great deal of effort but not learning to speak well. But why? Better books, specific goals and a classroom culture that can handle oral drills, which can easily get out of hand.

59. What is the building block method and what is the role of reading in this? In my experience, the best language teaching method is some form of the "building block method." There are many variations of this, but a typical first lesson uses the ten most basic words and explores every combination of ways to use them together. The next day the teacher might introduce five new words, and drill every combination of using them together. The old words are reinforced while introducing the new, and with slowly students build a core of the highest frequency words. This was the method of the Berlitz School.

60. What is a language course textbook that combines the best of language schools and the high school/college classroom? The *French in Action* series. I feel I owe it to my former French professor to mention that the best school course I ever took was Intensive Intermediate French, which used the so-called *French in Action* series. Features of that course included;

level appropriate readings
disciplined teacher - student oral drills
disciplined student - student oral drills
meticulous bookeeping by the professor
good listening assignments at the language lab
short, twice weekly writing assignments

* * *

8. Tandem Plus University of Minnesota Pomona College of Liberal Arts Language Center.
https://languagecenter.cla.umn.edu/tandem/
* * *

Table 3:
Levels of Student Language Ability

Achieving the levels of proficiency below requires that students read, which means using easy readers, which can be used with "frequency dictionaries", which assure students learn the highest frequency words. But, that's the technical side of things. The emotional benefits of spirited language study are also important.

Level 1	Students have *recognition* of up to 500 highest frequency words and basic grammar. The ability to use even the one hundred highest frequency words fluently makes conversation possible, something high school students that study a language for four years should be able to do.
Level 2	At least *recognition* of the core 500–1000 words, along with the most functional intermediate grammar. The post-World War Two German Chancellor Konrad Adenauer had an English vocabulary of about 600–700 words, but was able to talk comfortably with English speaking heads of state. For English language learners that are new to the U.S., this can be an exciting level, as communication and integration becomes easier.
Level 3	At least *recognition* of vocabulary of 1000–1500 words, most verb tenses and intermediate grammar. At this level you should be able to read some articles and *have the vocabulary* to understand most T.V. programs. English language learners students in the U.S. that get to this level will integrate into the classroom more easily, even if the knowledge is mostly passive.

61. What might be a better attitude regarding achieving proficiency? Testing can be informative of progress made and encourage effort, but the goal is effective communication in the target language. Not every student will get to level three in the chart on the previous page, but most that take Spanish for four years should be able to graduate from level one. What that means is the ability to have a conversation *and at least recognize* most vocabulary in level one easy readers.

Quality of Expression Some may recall the scene in the movie *The Dead Poets Society* in which there was an article on "defining poetry" by Dr. J. Evans Pritchard. (9) In that article, students were instructed to use a ruler to measure the poem and its value. That is of course ridiculous, as the value of poetry or any expression isn't best measured by the amount of grammar or vocabulary mastered alone. There is intrinsic value in mastery of a language through years of devoted study, but there is also value in expressing great ideas or acting as bridge builders between cultures, and this shouldn't be undermined by any test or ruler. As one jiu-jitsu master who had traveled and trained in Japan put it;

"Sometimes flashing a thumbs up sign while saying 'excellent' can open all sorts of new doors." (10)

62. What is the role of easy readers while teaching Spanish or German? When a teacher senses that the vocabulary of students is getting close to *at least recognition* of the three hundred highest frequency words, then one option is to start using easy readers. With an easy reader, the teacher can read simple stories and can ask comprehension questions as they go. This also works well in a classroom, because different students can read and the teacher can ask comprehension questions.

Spanish and Easy Readers Go Together Nicely

The Spanish grammar is easier than that of many other languages. What this means is that simple comprehension questions using easy readers are going to be much easier for students studying Spanish. If students can *at least recognize* the vocabulary, students studying Spanish can start reading easy readers sooner than in other languages, where the grammar can get confusing at even the beginner level.

* * *

9. Dead Poets Society, directed by Peter Weir (1989; Burbank, CA: Walt Disney Video, 1998) DVD

10. Jiu-jitsu definition: a japanese grappling art. Urban Dictionary, http://www.urbandictionary.com/define.php?term=jiu%20jitsu Testimonial; I feel I owe it to the jiu-jitsu world to testify as to the remarkable, powerful, positive effect that the practice of jiu-jitsu can have on people. Especially men. Myself, I am not even 1/3 of the way to my first belt, but have "rolled", or sparred quite a bit for someone in that position. Maybe a little south of 300 rounds. The potential that the art has for developing athletes is huge, as is how it might help those looking to constantly evolve their abilities to defend themselves in our rapidly changing world.

* * *

63. How important is is that good language learning happens for English language learners? The same way they are applied to learning any other language. This is important; because according to *MassINC.* (the original core source of this book), in my home state of Massachusetts 150,000 adults aged 18-64 speak little or no English. (11) With the right textbooks and systems, or just a great teacher, English language learners can advance steadily. Additionally, the Internet means that more learners can find language exchange partners online and exchange through Skype.

64. Why are the Blaine Ray books the easy reader of choice for many teachingSpanish? Students need a core vocabulary to begin reading, but the *Blaine Ray* books are written using only a fixed, controlled vocabulary. Many "easy readers" require a core vocabulary of 600 words to begin reading, whereas the easiest of the Blaine Ray books begin with a vocabulary of 300 words. It's difficult to get students up to a vocabulary of 600 words, especially when they can't read, because reading is the single best way to reinforce what has been learned.

What's important to remember with easy readers is that students only need to be able to recognize the core vocabulary to begin reading, as opposed to having the words fully memorized, which is much harder.

65. How are the "easy readers" organized at the French Library in Boston and why is this perfect? Not only there were excellent easy readers when I went into the *French Library* in Boston, but that library had the easy readers better organized than any other place I've ever been. (12) There were "250's", "500's" or "750's", organized into sections. That is what a really effective language program can have, books in sections written with the 250, 500 or 750 highest frequency words.

The benefits of easy readers in French are the same as in every other language; a review of core words and grammar while getting a better feel for the language.

66. What is another existing equivalent of vocabulary based easy readers? The ER Easy Reader series, although these books at least used to be way too hard to find. According to the website, "Easy Readers have a long and honourable history spanning nearly 70 years. The brainchild of a small Danish publishing house in the darkest years of the Second World War, the series now comprises more than 170 titles in six languages". Almost always good stories that create some atmosphere. they bring the language alive, and are organized by level.

Level A: written using the 600 highest frequency words.
Level B: written using the 750 highest frequency words. (13)

* * *

11. MassINC.

12. The French Library "houses the second largest collection of French books, periodicals, DVDs, and CDs available in the United States", at 53 Marlborough Street in Boston.

13. It needs to be said that the books and their core vocabulary numbers at least used to vary by language. For example, the French Library used to have French Level A books that were "250s", or written using the 250 highest frequency words. In contrast, Level A books in other languages would sometimes be written using a higher core vocabulary number.

* * *

67. What is the role of "graded readers"? Whereas easy readers are based on a fixed amount of vocabulary, such as being written using only the 300 highest frequency words, so-called "graded reader" tend to introduce a large amount of new vocabulary in order to tell a story. Search "Graded Spanish Reader"and you should find a few books for sale. Teachers naturally assign "graded reading"because they know where their class is at. Unlike so-called "easy readers" that require a minimum vocabulary to comprehend, graded readers can allow even beginners to begin reading, as the vocab and readings are tightly controlled.

    A. Reading Silently
    B. Reading out loud
    C. Reading out loud With emotion
    D. Reading in Rotation

68. What is the most practical application of all this core vocabulary, easy reader or graded reader talk? The most practical application would be the effective integration of recent arrivals to this country, and especially those struggling in school because of language barriers.

    A. Copying the Book
    B. Reading with Friends, Brothers or Sisters
    C. A teacher reads and asks comprehension questions
    D. A classmate reads and asks comprehension questions

69. Why do do some feel language classes should be a choice, and why do some sharply disagree?? Time in the classroom is valuable. Some feel that if students aren't up to doing the work involved in a language class, then they should find an activity they like better. Students in a second language class should want to be there. Some think a foreign language in high school is a good idea for 70–80% of students. However, some disagree sharply with that, as one Massachusetts language teacher expressed in a June 2022 letter to the *Boston Herald*. He felt that not only do all middle school students deserve a crack at learning a new language, but that it was important to making the schools in his district really work. He might be right.

70. How can making participation a large part of the final grade encourage students? For starters, it can give every student an avenue to success. In my experience, teachers vary from basing between ten to forty percent of the total grade on participation. There are many variables that go into choosing this number, but some believe basing a higher percentage of the grade on participation can help to improve classroom culture. Participation also encourages students to help out the weaker students, which is good.

71. What is the importance of a realistic syllabus in college language courses? In my experience, the syllabuses in college foreign language literature courses are often way too ambitious. For example, one French literature course assigned reading six or seven full books in French. Maybe one or two of the graduate students in the course might have been able to handle the reading, but for most of us it was just too much. Most of us would have been much better off reading one or two chapters of one book per week. That way we could have time to truly understand and digest all of the material.

Underutilized Skills and Knowledge? At the same time, how often does the extensive literary knowledge of professors go untapped because students are struggling just to understand the basics of the language? And what can we do about this? For starters, we can give teachers the support they need to be successful in the K-12 system.

72. What are some models for testing for credit? One model out there is testing for university credit. As it stands, if a student can pass an advanced placement exam in a language with a 3, 4 or 5, some colleges give the equivalent of one college course credit. A casual search revealed that the *University of Iowa* offers testing for credit in three ways:

> *Advanced Placement program*
> *International Baccalaureate Program and the*
> *College Level Examination Program.* (14)

The most practical. best known, or most mainstream of the three models above are arguably the AP, or Advanced Placement tests.

73. What is the future of language teacher training at community colleges? It certainly is one dimension of reviving town centers as places of learning and, in theory, to live out one Massachusetts' poet's dream of "making every village a university."(15) Using the map on pages 73, you can see the locations of these schools. In Massachusetts, for licensure, public school teachers have to pass two certification exams: one general literacy test and one test for his or her area of specialization. The best way I can describe the Spanish teacher certification exam is that it is like taking the SATs in Spanish. For some future teachers, finding a community college with the coursework required for certification near them might feel like spotting an oasis in the desert.

74. What's the role of college "language houses"? I remember one language house at Wesleyan University (16) in Connecticut: those people had a blast living and reaching their goals together. Students encouraged each other in their skill acquisition, practiced and learned to work together. At the end of the day that's what many people want; to work and connect with other people, to reach goals together.

* * *

14. The University of Iowa, undergraduate admissions.'
http://admissions.uiowa.edu/undergraduate/credit-exam-options
15. Thoreau, Henry David, "The Village", Walden; or Life in the Woods". Tinkner & Field. Boston 1854
16. Wesleyan University is a liberal arts college in Connecticut. Their Russian department is said to be one of the four or five best in the country. It is said that the little college was the favorite destination of Soviet era Russian writers, and that the often oppresed and tormented masters of the Russian language found comfort there, and treasured the memories of their visits.
* * *

75. What is the role of university and government cooperation? The 2003 International Studies in Higher Education Act began an era of the government giving money to university language programs, the idea being to "reflect national needs related to Homeland Security." (17) Harvard University was one recipient, with the Center for Middle Eastern Studies receiving $275,000 annually. The Asia Center receives $433,000 annually and the David Rockefeller Center for Latin American Studies averaging of $433,333 a year. (18) Funding was cut significantly, but the government money flowing to the private college is still significant. (19)

Language Programs and Peace In the meantime, one existing model for collaborative language learning is the "language scholar" program at Reed College, outlined in question eighty-four of this section. With global populations rising and wars and conflicts breaking out, people are going to need to listen and learn to each other, and the Reed College model can help with that. Perhaps affordable community and state colleges can learn from and apply the Reed model, and thereby do their part to contribute to effective language learning, and peace. (see question 85 on page 46)

76. What's a good example of college programs working hard to assure that students are systematically building vocabulary and learning to write? One is the approach of the Colorado St. German professor, who does it by assigning twenty-five to thirty word compositions. This is a good way to assure the "core word repetitions" learners need to build the base to comfortably communicate. (20) Asking students to be creative also means engaging more of their brain, which increases the value of the assignment. The 25-30 daily essay length is a good length for beginners, which allows them to focus on writing correctly.

77. What is the role of a "frequency dictionary" and how are they used in conjunction with "easy readers"? One system for building vocabulary is through a "frequency dictionary," a book that lists words in a language in the order of frequency in which they appear in a language. So, "word one" represents the single most common or frequent word in that language. And, "word two" is the second most common word in that language, and so on. What this means is that if you learn words 1-100, you will have mastered the one hundred most common words, or perhaps 30% of usage, which means you can begin to communicate.

The difference between using a frequency dictionary and learning random lists of words is that with a frequency dictionary you are assured to be learning the words you really need to know to be able to communicate.

* * *

17. Scarry, Joseph T., "Big Brother in Area Studies," The Harvard Crimson, December 5, 2003. www.thecrimson.com/
18. Ibid.
19. Ibid.
20. Colorado St. Gisela B. Estes, Barbara Lopez-Mayhew, Marie Therese Gardner, "Writing in the Foreign Languages Department," August 1998, http://wac.colostate.edu/journal/vol9/estes.pdf

* * *

Repetition, Repetition

Another key point with regard to frequency dictionaries is that learners need repetition in order to really get the words in their head. For that, they need to be able to read using those frequency words. The problem is it is incredibly difficult to read any books without a solid core vocabulary. In fact, to read even an easy book, you're going to need a vocabulary of at least 700 words or so. The number of words readers need to *recognize* for most books and magazines is about 1,200-1,500. This is the reason for easy readers.

78. What are some specific activities that students in college "language houses" do? Activities include; working with easy readers together, exchanges with native speakers in the house, or exchanges online. If it could vastly increase student learning. Easy readers are a very effective tool in the classroom, but they can also be very useful to two people studying together. One method for tutoring students in Spanish is to have the student doing the reading while the teacher asks comprehension questions on the text. Even fifteen minutes a day of that can increase learning exponentially.

Online Exchanges

As for online exchanges, students can sample the many different websites where prospective language partners meet and share their experiences with each other.

Housing for Adjuncts?

The potential that these language houses have for opening up housing opportunities to adjunct professors. After all, good language houses need a good leader and underpaid adjuncts might enjoy getting some free housing in exchange for supervising the house. This is especially true in my extremely expensive hometown Boston, but the principle is true anywhere in New England.

Maximizing Housing Dollars

The other relevant principle is that of students getting the most possible bang for their buck. That's to say that if parents or students are going to pay $10,000 or more per year for housing at the college, which at some of the more affordable colleges is almost as much as tuition, then they might consider getting some housing that added to the college experience and skills acquired.

79. Why were the Berlitz materials so effective? They were effective because they introduced a small amount of new material and reviewed the old with reading, writing and speaking. Each and every lesson had some readings that used only words that the students had been taught. With beginners, this is the key. The second series of books that really worked were those of the Blaine Ray, including *Pobre Ana* and *Ana Va a California*. (21) One of the best things to do for your language studies is to read, but the hard part is to get your vocabulary up to the point where reading is possible.

* * *

21. *Pobre Ana* and *Ana Va a California*, Blaine Ray Workshops
* * *

80. What is a good college language program that has rich content and advanced use of technology? One example is Spanish 311 at the College of Wooster, where Spanish playwrights make regular performances - - digitally. They also do face to face and class to class exchanges through Skype. Called "Contemporary Spanish Theatre in a Global Context," the model opens up many new doors, including adding a whole new dimension to "sister cities" and classrooms. (22) I also happen to know one Italian program does such a class to class program with a university in Italy. Clearly, there are more examples of this new trend, but that is one example.

81. What is the potential for exchanges between language classrooms in North and South America? Perhaps classrooms in the Americas will not only work together to do language exchanges, but students north and south of the border will learn from each other and work together. As communities struggle to preserve natural resources and unique ways of life, it's great when there is collaboration. For example, Costa Rica is a model of environmentalism, with about 25% of its land set aside for protection, and we as Americans might learn from that. As we seem to be utterly lacking in any kind of vision of conservation in the U.S., so we stand to learn and gain a great deal.

82. Why are online language exchanges so unique and valuable? Partnering with another student to practice languages is a good ways to progress, have fun and bring the language alive. And, because not everyone meets such a language partner during their college years, exchange websites can help facilitate these exchanges. Sometimes it can be even more effective than live tutoring. My experience learning Chinese from a teacher online taught me that with Skype and other programs it's possible to share the screen with the teacher. With a language like Chinese that is so difficult to read, sharing the screen means students can practice reading while the teacher listens and follows along. This is often more comfortable than sharing a book.

83. What is a good model for language partner facilitation? The University of Minnesota Tandem Plus program is one. (23) They organize three kinds of exchanges: face-to-face, virtual and class-to-class. Official policy states that; *"priority is given to language students currently enrolled in a class at the University of Minnesota, but registration is open to all."* So, when there is difficult finding an exchange partner for a student studying a more rarely studied language, (Urdu, Farsi or Swahili, for example) then perhaps someone could be found in the community for such an exchange. At the end of the day, what makes the TandemPlus program worth imitating is the low cost and high return.

* * *

22. "Technology Brings Spanish Playwrights into the Classroom," The College of Wooster News and Events, Feb. 27, 2013. www.wooster.edu/
23. Tandem Plus Pomona College of Liberal Arts Language Center. University of Minnesota, https://languagecenter.cla.umn.edu/tandem/

* * *

84. What is a good example of a college language house? The Reed College "language houses" are places where students can live and work together while speaking a foreign language. The Reed College model supports effective learning every fall. Eight so-called "language scholars" come or return to the college to act as mentors to students in the language houses. So, regardless of which of the five languages that students elect to study, there is a house where students can live and practice the language they're working on while interacting with current speakers outside their campus. (24)

85. How can we improve language teacher preparation? Teachers and professor and professor currently in the field might look at some of the existing successes profiled in this section. In the meantime, at some Massachusetts universities, they have an "MTEL Center,"(25) a place where students get help preparing for Massachusetts teacher certification exams. One article in the *Boston Herald* pointed out that graduates of University of Massachusetts at Dartmouth programs were particularly successful in passing teacher certification exams, with over 90% of graduates doing so. Is the curriculum constructed in such a way that students that simply do their work well for four years will naturally pass teacher certification exams? A theme to explore. For the record, MTEL stands for Massachusetts Testing for Educator Licensure.

However, because many schools are having a hard time attracting and retaining teachers, it is worth mentioning the value that reading out loud in your language of choice can add value to your studies. Students that hope to teach Spanish but do not test well can always add daily reading in Spanish while in school or as a group activity at a Spanish language house. Leadings those readings with peers can also be good practice for doing so professionally.

86. Can maximizing language programs assist with better attendance in high schools throughout the region? Many schools have a big problem with student attendance, and maximizing our language programs is one way to make school more interesting to students. As a seventh and eighth grader in the early eighties, I would have loved interactive language programs with my classmates, especially considering I was new to the city I also know many high school graduates that got excellent grades in Spanish, but they can barely speak the language, if at all. If I have learned one thing from twenty-seven years of teaching and studying languages, it's the value of reading out loud in the target language, at an appropriate reading level. I also know how incredibly rarely that is done.

* * *

24. Reed College Residence Life, www.reed.edu/res_life/on_campus/language_houses.html
25. MTEL (Massachusetts Testing for Educator Licensure) Test Preparation Resources, Salem State University.

* * *

Dimensions of Effectively Reading Out Loud
Recognition of at least 70% of vocabulary
Expression of a wide range of emotions
Go full theatrical Shakespeare if it pleaseth thee

Benefits of Effectively Reading Out Loud
Massive repetition of vocabulary
Massive repetition of grammar in context
In some cases, connecting with your roots

Table 4
Language Departments Adapt

New technology means that students, language departments and adult students have many new learning opportunities and ways to learn. How new or existing models can be realized at community colleges is one focus of this chapter.

Reading Out Loud	*Let it Fly!* Reading out loud in the target language can lead to daily progress and bring the language alive. There is no better way to reinforce core vocabulary or grammar basics. Near theatrical readings of simple texts can be a great learning tool for energetic students.
The Role of New Technology	*A. Online Exchanges* One-on-one exchanges can be good practice for students and a great way for adults to practice & connect. *B. Classroom to Classroom Exchanges.* One Italian class does live classes between the U.S. and Italy. *C. Internet Radio* Radio can be sampled in the classroom. *D. Course Equivalency Tool* Credits are now more easily transferred from school to school, which opens up new possibilities.
Community Colleges: Opportunity Knocks	*A. Tandem Plus Model* Schools in areas with migrants or foreign students have a pool of potential exchange partners. *B. Sharing Screens* Few students read out loud in the target language. The University of Minnesota *Tandem Plus* model can help.
Language House Models	A. The Reed College language house "visiting scholars" program (Oregon) creates golden learning opportunities for all. B. Wesleyan University in Connecticut has special interest housing, including language houses, that are worthy of study.
Connecting the Blind?	A prime example of a group that can benefit greatly from exchanges is the blind. Learning a language as a blind person has special challenges, but also special benefits. A blind student learning English practicing with a blind American learning Spanish online: priceless.

Crop Mob in Vermont. Students volunteer to help farmers who might be under-staffed to help keep food costs low for families and continue the support for local farming.

87-110:
Progressive Coursework Models

"Throughout modern history, students have been the engine that powers the most transformative of movements. From civil rights to women's rights, students acted as catalysts for earth shifting change."

Guide to Transforming your Campus, Community and Career, U.S. Green Building Council (1)

87. What are some existing measures of how "green" a college is? Before beginning reading the chapter on progressive coursework, I'll share what I see as progressive, because people have different ideas of what that is. For me, three main categories of "progressive"; job creation, or coursework that gives people of all economic backgrounds a future, progress in the green revolution and responding to three major weak points in our push towards sustainability.

Job Creation
Paths of study that lead to employment, such as apprenticeships, industry partnerships, farm jobs or other jobs of the future are promoted. The first focus here is that students of any background might find a path to employment, and to look at the labor force participation rate, as well as the different unemployment rates. To be truly inclusive, we need to have *accounting for everyone*.

The Green Revolution
By "Green Revolution" I mean supporting local farms, building our network of walking and bike paths, recycling, renewable energy and more. In short, some of the ways you probably imagine as "green".

Addressing the "Big Three" Weak Points
I see our three big failures as reduction of animal cruelty, the failure to develop a conservationist vision and the failure to respond to species extinction. I go after all three of these issues, but I pursue animal cruelty with a particular vigor. Truth be told, in my view, true progressivism involves standing up for the "Big Three", as I call them.

There really is no one standard definition of "sustainability", "green" or anything else, but a lot of good work has been done to define this. Typically, when magazines or websites judge how "green" a college is, the criteria may include the number of solar panels, recycling or if they are "carbon neutral." However, the table on the next page provides a wide variety of existing measures for us to learn from.

* * *

1. "Guide to Transforming your Campus, Community and Career", U.S. Green Building Council http://buildingfree.com/pages/12880564-usgbc-students-toolkit-guide-to-transforming-your-campus.

* * *

Table 5:

Existing Measures of Green Colleges

For supporters of New England colleges looking for them to go green.

Four Existing Models of Measuring "Greenness"	*Princeton Review of Green Colleges* With 62% of students expressing interest in attending "green" colleges, the Princeton Review ranks colleges' "greenness" on six criteria. The *CS Best Practices Manual* is an easy-to-use guide for schools to capitalize on green energy opportunities on campus. The *Wesleyan 2016 Best Practices Manual* is a five year, multidimensional plan for building a green, healthy campus. The *College of the Atlantic* youtube channel is a good model that showcases its work in Human Ecology well. Human Ecology is "the study of the effect of humans on the planet".
AASHE	The American Association of Sustainability in Higher Education is a leader in the nuts and bolts of building green campuses. - Their website www.aashe.org has many tools. - Their organizations provides leadership on 326 campuses. - They use 17 "distinct aspects of defining sustainability".
Green College Weak Points: A-D	A. *Animal Cruelty* For real progress in reducing animal cruelty, the efforts of *The National Humane Education Society* is a group who should be analyzed in the classroom. **See:** The NHES and Factory Farms: https://nhes.org/3372-2/ B. *Conservation* One weak point is promotion of a conservationist vision. This is relevant to "species extinction", as alteration of habitat is one cause of the devastation of animal species C. *Food Waste* 1/3 of food being wasted on campus means needless animal suffering. See "Lawrence among Top Twenty Schools Nation-wide for Recycling Efforts." by Emily Zawacki for responses. D. *Extinction* "Conservation Biology (CB) courses, taught worldwide at universities, typically focus on the proximal causes of extinction without teaching students how to respond to the crisis" See: "Education as a tool for addressing the extinction crisis: moving students from understanding to action" by Lucas Moyer-Horner in *PubMed*.

88. How much food does the college buy from local producers? Buying food from local farms means a relationship with the farm of origin. That relationship with also means the university can better meet the health needs of students, not to mention insisting on the humane treatment of animals or not using pesticides.

Colleges can boost to local farmers by supporting farmer's markets orbuying shares of community-supported agriculture. Buying their produce locally can boost local economies, give students the food they need to feel their best and prevent disease and create summer agricultural employment.

Greenfield CC Farm and Food Systems Program Within Massachusetts, one university actively participating in the local economy is the Greenfield Community College *Farm and Food Systems* program. The program at GCC has a great habit of visiting other agricultural programs and applying the lessons learned back home.

89. Do students and faculty participate in crop mobs? "Crop mobbing" is a good way for students to connect with local farms. Groups go help farmers with their crops in return for a tour and maybe a good lunch after a morning's work. Mob jobs can include weeding, harvesting or any job done well by many hands.

In Vermont, the Green Mountain Crop Mob is now linked with the University of Vermont Center for Sustainable Agriculture. Farmers can request to be put on the list through the UVM website, and students can sign up to be contacted about joining one of the mobs. It's a win-win situation for everyone.

90. Is the food served at the college organic *and* humane? By serving organic food on campus, community members are getting more nutrients and eating foods with fewer hormonal additives. Also, they are promoting more environmentally-friendly farming methods and potentially better treatment of livestock.

The Lesson of No Impact Man Buying certified, animal-friendly and organic products means that it is *more likely* that the animals were raised humanely and not fed drugs or hormones. I learned this from *No Impact Man,*(2) in which the main character takes the train to upstate New York to see a farm and understand how the food is grown. In the documentary, the farmer emphasized to not judge entirely according to how "organic" food is labeled. Instead, he said you have to come see the animals for yourself to see how they're being treated.

The only example of a New England class going to see how the animals are treated I was able to find was a "Capstone Class" at one school that visited two slaughterhouses, which I read about in the school paper *The Argo*.(3) Many might say young people shouldn't be exposed to this, but I think we need to face the consequences of our actions. For this reason, kudos to this class.

* * *

2. No Impact Man 2009. Directors; Laura Gabbert and Justin Schein. IMDb
3. Larry Gu and Alicia Zou, "Senior Capstone Class Visits Slaughterhouse," *The Argo*, Page 3

* * *

What does "organic" mean? Organic farming is a return to farming that took place before the 19th and 20th century, a production method that better sustains the health of soils, ecosystems and people. Whereas modern agriculture would utilize artificial fertilizer, organic farms utilize crop rotation and "cover crops," planted to help to assure soil fertility and sustainability. Organic farmers emphasize weed suppression rather than weed killing pesticides, and avoid chemicals to combat pests. (4)

91. What percentage of energy used on campus in produced by the college? A growing number of schools and colleges produce some of their own power from solar panels, solar water heaters, wind turbines and other mechanisms. A good example of this kind of reliance is Butte College in Northern California, which in 2011 became the first American college to be "grid positive;" producing more electricity than it consumes. The 25,000 solar panels produce a surplus that can power hundreds of homes as well. Even better, the college is on track to save millions in energy costs down the road. (5) Of course not every college has access to the solar radiance of Northern California, but every school can work toward the their own goals.

92. How is the recycling program? Most campuses have recycling programs, but some incorporate elements that other campuses do not, such as recycling steel. One way to measure how well schools are doing is to participate in the annual RecycleMania competition. Success is measured in part by "recyclable pounds per person," with each college getting a rating. The feedback from this friendly competition can help lead to idea sharing and advancements in recycling. (6)

Ideally, analysis of the effectiveness of the recycling program and analyses can reduce waste. It can include looking at how leaves and other yard waste is recycled on campus grounds, or how all three words involved in increasing utilization of resources are implemented campus-wide: reduce, reuse, recycle. That said, see question 113 on page 65 shares how the New England leaders in recycling do things.

93. Are there common spaces where students can grow vegetables or engage in other forms of permaculture? Some people never had the opportunity to learn how to grow vegetables, but everyone should have a chance to learn how to grow fruits and vegetables without chemical fertilizers or synthetic pesticides. After all, vegetable gardens produce the food that can preserve health and save families money.

One example of permaculture at college is the work of *Wild Wes* at Wesleyan University in Connecticut. Working with the administration, students worked to convert an area of lawn into a combination of trees and flowers. It should be noted that such clubs can experience a boost from the American Association of Sustainability in Higher Education, or AASHE, as one of their roles is to support "green" clubs as they transition from year to year and in summers, which can be challenging.

* * *

4. "Nutrition and Healthy Eating," Mayo Clinic, December 3, 2011- www.mayoclinic.com
5. Stephen Messenger, "College in California Becomes First to Produce More Energy Than It uses," TreeHugger, June 30, 2011.
6. Emily Zawacki, Recyclemania. The Lawrentian
* * *

94. Are students and faculty engaged in the discussion surrounding the exploration of and creation of new national parks? This question is here because I don't believe we have a vision of conservation for the country or New England, but we need one. Perhaps students would be delighted to take part in this conversation.

In about 2005 I looked at a map of existing national parks within the U.S., and was struck by how small of an area they cover., and how few of them were in the eastern U.S., and it was striking how little discussion there was of this in college Environmental Science websites that I visited. This is a problem, but also an opportunity.

The dysfunctional, politically based debate in Maine over the creation of the Katadhin National Monument further demonstrated that we need new voices engaged in discussions on conservation. The creation of a national monument or national park should be a source of excitement and joy for Americans, and not be yet one more subject to disagree upon. In a nutshell, professors, outdoor enthusiasts, students, engineers and others have a lot to offer in coming up with a plan to protect the wild places of New England, so future generations can enjoy them.

95. What is an affordable New England college that is perfectly positioned to be a leader in green, progressive programs? Johnson St. College in Vermont. As is discussed in question 94, while doing some research on science coursework in New England, I noticed that very few departments were active in the discussion surrounding the creation or maintenance of new parks. Johnson State College in Vermont (which merged with Lyndon State to become Northern Vermont University in 2018) is one New England institution that is responding to serious long-term ecological questions within their Environmental and Health Sciences Department. As the web page of that department states; (7)

"students take on the challenges of a growing population, limited energy and climate change while taking courses in six different sciences."

The tuition and mandatory fees for Johnson State are low for Vermont residents, so as they continue to evolve and respond to the challenges in conservation, climate change, and other understudied themes, the soft glow of that jewel of the north can brighten the lives of yet more New Englanders.

96. Is there any connection between college science programs and renewable energy groups? Another way to activate connections between young minds and conservation groups is through internships. For example, George Mason University offers a minor in Renewable Energy, and students are required to complete an internship with a renewable energy group or company. In this way, students acquire practical knowledge and group they work for gets some needed help. (8)

* * *

7. Environmental Science Web Page, Johnson State College.
www.jsc.edu/academics/environmental-health-sciences/majors/environmental-science
8. "Renewable Energy Minor," George Mason University College of Science, accessed May 10, 2012,
http://cos.gmu.edu/academics/undergraduate/minors/renewable-energy

* * *

97. Is the school community active in measuring soil quality, composting and waste? Through our choices we affect the value of our soil, water and air quality, greenhouse gases and the sustainability of land productivity. (9) One example of such an institution that works on these things is the Cornell Waste Management Institute, which *"provides training for students in multidisciplinary approaches to bringing university resources to bear on solving waste management problems."* (10) Offering short courses and workshops for government officials, waste industry people and the public, the CWMI is a model for sustainability.

98. Is research on supporting quality of life for older, disabled or other vulnerable Americans available on college YouTube channels? Afer having spent about 500 hours on New England college Youtube channels, I saw very few videos that explored ways to increase quality of life for older Americans. However, one video was a University of New Hampshire video showing a workout with an older woman, in which a student and faculty member worked together with an older woman to help her learn how to workout. Another video from University of Maine video shows the development of a wheelchair by students and faculty that could move well on rough terrain, which means that those in wheelchairs are not restricted to paved surfaces.

99. What are some existing efforts to create 20,000 jobs in the city? In an article by Christian Triunfo titled "Walsh Implements New Program to Create New Jobs", published in the *The Huntington News* in 2018, a quote of note was; *"among his many inauguration promises was the establishment of Boston Hires, a city led effort that aims to place 20,000 unemployed or underemployed Bostonians in jobs that pay a living wage."* For the record, City Hall defines a living wage as $14.41 an hour. Groups mentioned in that article involved in job creation efforts include:

> *Building Pathways, a pre-apprenticeship program*
> *Boston Local Initiatives Support Coalition*
> *Boston's Operation A.B.L.E., a training service for workers over 45.*

Creating 20,000 jobs in any city is hard, but the following paragraphs highlight some existing, successful efforts.

The Role of Community Colleges

Table 9 on page 86 focuses on the role community colleges in job creation, including apprenticeships, industry partnerships and manufacturing. Three models include those at; York County Community College, Vermont Technical College and Great Bay Community College (NH). Other existing New England models are on page 89. Existing successes of community colleges are on the table on page 86.That said, of course there are many other pockets of opportunity and models that might become a source of jobs in Boston.

* * *

9. "Value of Soil," Soil Quality for Environmental Health, last updated September 19, 2011, http://soilquality.org/basics/value.html
10. Cornell Waste Management Institute, accessed June 11, 2012, http://cwmi.css.cornell.edu/about-wmi.html

* * *

The Contributions of Quinsigamond Community College

In an interview entitled "Shop Talk"with the *Worcester Business Journal,* Jack Healy of the Massachusetts Extension Partnership was asked the question: "What would you say is the one thing that manufacturing in this state needs in order to grow?", to which he said: "an educated workforce". He went on to say many other informative things about manufacturing in Central Massachusetts, but prime among them is that Quinsigamond Community College was doing an outstanding job in supporting manufacturers and the manufacturing community with their programs. The larger question is whether or not the Quinsigamond model would work in Boston.

The highly informative Jack Healy MEP video was posted on the youtube page of "WBJEditor" on 9/29/2014. The extended interview is at wbjournal.com.

Support the Disabled, Support the Economy

The process of supporting the disabled can help us find solutions to questions of job creation. Pages 98-101 focus on the disabled and the Massachusetts economy.

The Plight of Adjuncts

Many adjunct professors live and work in Boston, and the fact that college enrollment nationwide may continue to drop could lead to cuts in faculty, as was in danger of happening to 400 adjuncts at the UMass Boston in early 2017. Colleges going out of business is another issue, and is the subject of question 103. Pages 31-32 focus on existing supports of New England adjuncts.

STEM Jobs

Standing for Science, Technology, Engineering and Math, STEM jobs representing many of the jobs of the future, and pages 114-118 goes into that. However, of any point made in that chapter that relates to the goal of job creation, the table in the informative article by Steve Lohr on page 116 is a great place to start. Local new STEM programming includes the STEM program at Massachusetts Bay Community College and the creation of a school of engineering at Boston College in 2019.

Job Creation and the Minimum Wage

Since 2018, the former Boston Mayor moved to the national stage, and focusing on maximizing existing jobs through raising the federal minimum wage. If one thing needs to be said on that subject, it is that the quality of the talking and the listening on this subject needs to be a little higher than in past decades. Industry experts, suffering workers and struggling employers all need to be heard.

100. Is there any engagement between students and local "Safe Routes," "rail trail" or walking groups? Like many others, spending time on "rail trails" has been a source of healthy recreation. And, realizing the dream of a network of connected trails throughout New England is something that the younger generation might enjoy participating in. The walk-to-school models pioneered by *Safe Routes* are arguably the easiest programs for students to get involved in. One way to get involved is to check out the *Safe Routes* website, which has case studies, or to look at the page for parents to learn about "walking school buses".

101. How might a resurgence in high school and college radio create community? Having had a show at a college radio station for six years, I learned some things, and I can say that it can really help.

College Radio is Fresh and Relaxing I'll never forget the first time I listened to WMWM, 91.7 FM on the way home. One of the long time shows on that college station was *Rats in the Oven* and it was on. The music was absolutely not my taste, and the talk a bit silly. But you know what? *It was authentic*, and soon I found myself really chilled out, which in turn made me enjoy the show more. We are living in a time when this kind of authenticity can be invaluable to a lot of people.

Piping in to Common Areas is Key Back in the day, WZBC, 90.3 FM used to pipe their radio into the Eagle's Nest, a common area for students. Having a common area where the station is broadcast is a great way to reach and ideally engage students with their community radio culture.

Incidentally, it was right about the time that Boston College defeated Alabama in football two years in a row, in 1983 and 1984, when I was on campus with a family member with some frequency. Down 31-14 in the 3rd quarter, B.C. rallied back to win 38-31, with Troy Stratford's 42 yard run in the 4th sealing it. There was something special in the air those years, and I felt it as I walked by the *Eagle's Nest* at that time. Those days may be over, but maybe not forever. (11)

Student Run Radio is Essential Whether we like to admit it or not, as we get older we often get less fun, less creative, crankier and more set in our ways. What this means is that after six years in college radio, I can say that it's essential that the students run the show. Some college stations are blessed with adult staff that assist in running the station, and they can contribute in huge ways, but in my experience shows are much fresher without too much adult interference.

Engaging in Conservation Talk and Much More This book points out a few areas, which don't get nearly enough attention, and college radio can respond. Whether it's countering animal cruelty (See Table 5 on page 52 and Table 7 page 68), reversing species extinction or constructing a conservationist vision for New England, college radio can add a lot to the discussion.

So, a few of the possibilities of school and colleges radio are above, but doyou know what? The truth is the best shows on radio are often about small but entertaining subjects. In fact, the first show broadcast in common areas could be on a subject as simple as about what kind of coffee they should serve in the dining hall.

* * *

11. "BC Alabama Football 1984", Youtube Video, John Fidler.
www.youtube.com/watch?v=XCExyGFkysc

* * *

102. Is there a solar water heater on campus and do students know how it works? Solar water heaters are great money and energy savers, but choosing the right one requires some knowledge. There are active and passive solar water heater systems, solar panel water heaters and solar energy water heaters to choose from, and schools can help introduce to them in their class work.

Widely used in China, Japan, Greece, Australia, Turkey, Israel and European Union countries, solar heaters still make up a tiny percentage of the market here in the states. (12) And, although passive systems easily gather energy in sunny states like California, colder climates require an active system, necessitating a passive system with circulation pumps and controls. Currently, installation costs are high, however heating our water from the sun's power would take a great deal of power off the grid. Greater use of the devices, which will in turn lower costs and unclean energy consumption.

For parents, students and educators in New England looking for course models or opportunities that respond to the need for more solar, the course *Intro to Solar PV* at Vermont Technical College is the most practical model I've been able to find. It is designed for two kinds of students: 1) those looking to become a Solar technician or 2) those just looking to learn how to work on their own home.

103. Why is the demise of Green Mountain College and important case study to learn from? A beautiful, dynamic, beloved, unique Vermont college with passionate students, faculty and alumni closed its doors forever. That alone warrants use of one of the questions in this book to address that. Except, I have already been down that road with all the other questions in this book. So, in this case, it is left to readers to figure out what might have been done differently, and how the 200+ remaining colleges in New England might respond.

See: "It's Just Really Sad: Green Mountain Students, Faculty Respond to Closure", on *Vermont Public Radio* (Keck, 2019) (13)

104. Does the college utilize or promote electric and hybrid vehicles? The transition to greater use of electric or hybrid cars can be helped through coursework on the inner workings of the vehicles, as well as on-campus displays. California State University at Monterrey Bay uses twenty electric scooters for parking enforcement and campus safety, which is one way to promote 'clean' vehicles on campus. Colleges can combine this with presentations on campus, "outdoor showroom style," something I'm sure the auto makers would be happy to do and that students would enjoy. (14) In the case of California it offered tax credits, rebates and access to the carpool lane. California State also installed two electric vehicle charging stations, something that has since been adopted at at least one Massachusetts state college.

* * *

12. Phillipe Menanteau, "Policy Measures to Support Solar Water Heating: Information, Incentives and Regulations," World Energy Council, May 2007. www.worldenergy.org/documents/solar_synthesis.pdf
13. *Vermont Public Radio* It's Just Really Sad: Green Mountain Students, Faculty Respond to Closure". (Keck, 2019)
14. "Newly Installed Stations to Charge up Electric Vehicles," Cal State LA, accessed June 11, 2012, www.calstatela.edu/

* * *

105. Do college YouTube channels have videos on green energy initiatives, conservation or other positive steps? In 2016, I did a survey of the YouTube channel of every New England college that I could find. The reason I started to look was to build a playlist of videos on New England conservation, New England farming, green energy and local economy initiatives. What I found was that there were quite a few initiatives on these subjects, but that not so many of them came from the college websites. In the realm of local farming, there were some good videos from the University of Maine and the University of Massachusetts School of Agriculture. Greenfield Community College has a particularly good YouTube channel, with many videos reflective of the commitment of that college to be an integral part of the local economy and farming.

The College of the Atlantic Of any college in New England, the YouTube channel I enjoyed the most was that of the College of the Atlantic. Whereas the channels of many schools consist largely of admissions, a campus tour and sports videos, the College of the Atlantic channel features lectures and presentations that reflect the commitment of the Bar Harbor, Maine college to their sole major—human ecology. The two categories of videos that make the channel unique are "senior project presentations" and "featured lectures." The senior project presentations were awesome, reflecting the passions of the student body and the raw beauty of neighboring Acadia National Park.

Some guest lectures were also featured, from Amy Goodman to a man that did a fine job telling the tale of the history of French architecture in the area near Acadia National Park.

106. Does the college offer coursework in STEM., and do they explain where the jobs are and are not? It is said that jobs in STEM, which stands for Science, Technology, Engineering and Math represent a significant chunk of the jobs of the future, although the opportunities within the different fields vary widely. This is why pages 114-118 are devoted to this subject, and that section is highly informative.

Guidance and STEM The only point not made in pages 114-118 is that it is not enough to offer coursework in STEM fields. Rather, students need to understand where the jobs are and where they are not, and guidance counseling can help with that. With regards to STEM readers might check out pages 114-118, which is all about STEM. However, to understand all of the choices regarding STEM programming and employment, students need the latest information. One example of that is the table on STEM education and employment from the Steve Lohr article on page 116: that article and table are from 2017, and things may change.

107. Is there a course that studies the current state of ocean fish populations? In the words of the Pew Charitable Trust, *"fishermen, conservationists and scientists have actively debated how best to manage our ocean fish populations for decades. But with so much at stake, it's critical that as many Americans as possible be actively engaged in this discussion."* (15) This sounds great, but I've had little success finding any courses on this subject. Perhaps the minds of students can bring fresh new energy and perspectives to the debate.

* * *

15. Lee Crockett, "Overfishing 101: A Beginner's Guide to Understanding U.S. Fishery Management," The Pew Charitable Trusts. March

* * *

108. Are there courses that focus on reducing our dependence on foreign oil? Reliance on foreign oil causes many problems, one of which is that when dealing with conflict in Middle Eastern countries we can't be completely objective because we need their oil. If we could become energy self-sufficient, then we just might be able to be leaders in any peace process. The question is: are there colleges that focus on how we can shake that dependence?

There are a few possible angles that colleges can take to promote a reduction in oil dependence. There is a lot of talk about the need for a national energy policy, but perhaps we can best reach our goals by working at the state level, for two reasons. First, wind, sun and hydro resources vary a great deal from state to state. Second, we might do well to allow each of the fifty states to see what kind of plan they can come with. Just as our federalist system can be useful in comparing health care delivery, so too might it be in renewable energy.

109. Do students study the German energy model and what is a New England response? Wind energy accounts for a mere 1% of the electricity produced in the United States, although some believe we can get this number to 20%. (16) However, Germany's progress in renewable energy is worth noticing, where the amount of electricity produced from renewables has increased from 6.3 percent in 2000 to 25% in 2012. The enactment of the German Renewable Energy Act also provided a major boost to renewable energy in the often rainy, not so windy country. Perhaps the study of legislation like this could yield information we could apply here in the U.S., especially in areas with a lack of wind and solar.

On May 8, 2016, due to an extraordinary amount of energy produced from the sun and wind, there was a surplus of energy, more than could be stored. As a result, Germans were actually *paid* to consume energy. (17) This bodes well for the future of green energy, should these outcomes be replicated.

For parents, students and educators in New England looking for course models or opportunities *now,* the course *Intro to Solar PV* at Vermont Technical College is the most practical model I've been able to find for those looking to become a Solar technician or just to learn how to work on their own home.

110. Do students learn about U.S. wildlife policy or conservation efforts? Wildlife decisions made every day have a big impact on animal life. For example, wildlife officials kill about one million animals per year as part of "predator control" policy. (18) One aspect of this conversation is looking at the implications of the comeback of some animal species, such as the bison on the Great Plains. Will the rumbling herds not seen since the 1800's again inhabit our grasslands? This may sound crazy, but there is a movement to bring the bison back and make the plains into a national park, which is the theme of *American Serengeti,* hosted by Tom Selleck. A takeaway quote from that film is:

> *"Current conservation efforts are attempting to connect three million acres of grasslands to restore the ecosystem."*

* * *

16. "Wind Energy: Lesson Plans and Resource Guide," EFMR Monitoring Group
17. May 8th Germany, Fortune, http://fortune.com/2016/05/11/germany-excess-power/
18. See National Parks Map, www.nps.gov/nps/customcf/apps/park-search/img/nat-map-final-1208.jpg

* * *

According to the website of the *Buffalo Bill Center of the West*, "the film's screening at the Center of the West fittingly coincides with this year's National Bison Day, recently designated by the U.S. Senate." Even talking about the recreation of such a national preserve is a massive step forward for the American environmental movement, and teachers and students might enjoy being a part of learning about this. (20)

National Park Expansion Exploring the potential for expanding protected areas and national parks in the mid-west and east is an area of particular focus, because the majority of land reserves are in the south and mid-west. The problem is that with the growing population of our country, setting aside vast tracts of land becomes increasingly difficult. This is especially true in the mid-west and east, where humans are numerous. (21)

"The American Serengeti" in the American Great Plains, which would be a giant step forward for American environmentalism. Currently, a number of groups are patching together a number of different tracts of land in an effort to recreate the wildlife-filled plains that Lewis and Clark discovered two hundred years ago. Student groups that learned about this could be a blessing to existing efforts by groups such as the American Plains Group. (22) In the meantime, the story of Sagamore Hill on the next page is a smaller project closer to home to learn about.

* * *

20. *American Serengeti,* directed by Andy Mitchell (2010 : Montana: National Geographic Television), DVD *American Serengeti* was narrated by Tom Selleck about the creation of a National Park on the American Great Plains.
21. Ibid.
22. Ibid.

* * *

111-117
Promoting Conservation and Fighting Animal Cruelty

"The Wampanoag tribe laboratory MA is also developing groundwater, wetland, vernal pool, and sediment sampling protocols to better understand the wider hydrology and aquatic biology of the region".

- Wampanoag tribe MA of Aquinnah website

111. What is a Massachusetts model for future park creation? Due to the relatively small size of Massachusetts compared to other states, we don't have the large national parks that some states do. Nonetheless, we do have 356 state parks.(1) That said, it is encouraging to see the example of an attempt at national park creation in early 2016 of a 305 acre national park in Hamilton, Massachusetts.

The noble efforts toward park creation are significant in two ways; the obvious value of more park space and the opportunities for studying the model. As for the opportunities for learning from the model, the questions to be asked and answered are many, which are exemplified on the chart on the next page.

Sagamore Hill on the old Donovan property in Hamilton
MA is trying to become a small national park.

* * *

1. Energy and Environmental Affairs. www.mass.gov/eea/agencies/dcr/massparks/places-to-go/massachusetts-state-parks-alpha.html

* * *

Table 6:

On Campus Dimensions of State or National Park Creation

After following the debate surrounding the creation of the national park in Maine, it was striking how incomplete that discussion was. Eventually, the Katadhin region was declared a national monument via executive order, but perhaps the people would be better served with a more complete discussion that includes local and regional papers, local authors, environmental groups, and college professors.

Local Papers and Student Journalism	1. Do local papers give voice to area residents and their hopes for the park? 2. Are high schools included? A thoughtful and engaged high school student beats a know-it-all college student anyday. 3.Do student newspapers or journalism students write about environmental efforts students are involved in?
Climate Change and Parks	1. Can science departments concerned with climate change (Johnson State et al) put their weight behind park creation? 2.Parks create oxygen from carbon. See: The article "Top 5 Picks for New National Parks" in Travellers' Magazine.
Conservation and Reversing Species Extinction	1. Conservation is one aspect of reversing species extinction, and that might be included in public park discussions. Example: the "piping plover" in Massachusetts and Maine. 2. According to *Threatened Animals Worldwide, A Familiar Pocket Guide to Familiar Species,* the five threats to species are: Loss of Habitat Human Conflicts Wildlife Trade Commercial Fishing and Bycatch Global Warming. 3. Gordon College and many others have a sign telling the story of a conservation area with a "scan it barcode" for people to look up the protected species of that space. A good model! 4. See: Sudbury Valley Trustees MA for a model of RCP, or regional conservation partnership engagement with all ages. 5. Are tribal contributions such as those in question 114 recognized and discussed? 6. Has anyone read the paper of Lucas Moyer-Horner on conservation biology and species extinction?

112. Did New England Colleges discuss the proposed new national park in Maine? The proposed Maine North Woods national park is incredibly exciting; it would represent the first major new national park in New England in a long time. It also represents an effort to preserve the environment and long-term well-being of our home region.

A start to understanding is to have a look at a video put out by Lee Ann Szelog, in which she does a great job highlighting the need for the park. At a time when we are bombarded with images of decay, fear and war, it would be nice for the younger generation to take part in creating something awesome. In the meantime, returning veterans can learn about opportunities to link the discussion through the Veterans Conservation Corp., which places returning veterans in conservation jobs.(2)

113. How might the "waste audit" at the College of the Atlantic be the gold standard of effective use of resources, and be one for others to learn from? An article on recycling in *The Lawrentian* on Recylemania did a great job of comparing and praising the successes of different schools, but the College of the Atlantic is at another level. The value of the "waste audit" at the COA is that they calculate the exact amount of waste in each category. (3) The goal of the audit is : "Collecting data of College of the Atlantic waste over a week to educate and inform change". It could be argued that the process of the COA waste audit is the most complete approach to being responsible for our actions.

"Remember, reduce, reuse, repair, redesign, remake, rethink, reach out, research. And then you recycle".

College of the Atlantic student

114. What should New England students know about the contributions of New England Native American groups to conservation? Many Native American groups are working hard toward great environmental goals, whether it is bringing back the bison to the Plains or becoming energy self-sufficient. Tribal colleges with green energy curriculum adds a whole new range of possibilities for reconnecting Native American tribes and their perspective. One Massachusetts example of native tribes engaging in research worthy of classroom study is the monitoring of water quality that the Wampanoag tribe laboratory performs in Aquinnah, Martha's Vineyard. The laboratory:

"is also developing groundwater, wetland, vernal pool, and sediment sampling protocols to better understand the wider hydrology and aquatic biology of the region".

* * *

2. Veteran Conservation Corps. www.corpsnetwork.org/impact conservation/veterans-conservation-corps

3. Youtube Video, College of the Atlantic Campus Waste Audit, 2014. The College of the Atlantic in Bar Harbor, Maine is unique in many ways, but one of those ways is that they only offer one major, Human Ecology, which is essentially the study of the effect of humans on every aspect of the planet.

* * *

This is clearly a highly useful role, especially considering the fact that data is compiled and analyzed with an eye to how it will impact quality of life in the future.

115. Are there courses for learning about expanding our walking and bike path network? Building and expanding upon existing walking and bike paths requires local people with extensive knowledge of engineering, politics and planning. However, if these goals are reached, they not only provide people with healthy walking options, but they are also great places to give pets exercise. Colleges that offer Pedestrian, Bike and Information Center coursework include the University of California – Berkeley, Portland State University, the University of Washington, the Harvard School of Public Health, West Virginia University, UCLA, Skidmore College, Texas State, Prescott College, the University of Oregon, Temple University, Augsburg College and the University of Chicago. (4)

HSPH: The Lone Wolf In New England, as of 2013, the Harvard School of Public Health is the only school in New England that offers the PBIC (Pedestrian, Bike and Information Center) coursework. Communities looking to have more walking and bike infrastructure for both people and dogs are lucky to have someone that has taken the course and done the PBIC coursework.

116. Do students learn about ways to reduce with the large numbers of cats and dogs being killed in shelters? Probably not. The next generation needs to do better than we have in a number of areas, including reducing animal cruelty, engaging in conservation and reversing species extinction. With over 200 colleges in New England, at a time of declining enrollment, and a pressing need of some schools to remain relevant or even solvent, this is arguably an area of opportunity.

The PBS Movie According to the movie *Shelter Me* on PBS, the reason 3-4 million dogs are being killed in shelters every year is that breeders are producing too many animals, not enough are spayed and people tend not to go to shelters when getting dogs. According to the same movie on the subject, the solution is to put restrictions on breeders, neuter cats and dogs from shelters, counter myths about shelters and place them in more attractive locations. (5)

One Philosophy Department Responds One University of Redlands philosophy course (not in New England) visited a number of shelters to look at ways to reduce the number of kills. (6) One of the shelter's missions the class visited is to prevent animal cruelty and educate and help people care for animals in a responsible way.

* * *

4. Pedestrian, Bike and Information Center
5. Shelter Me; Let's Go Home, PBS
6. Molly Davis, "Bulldogs Study Shelter Dogs during May Term." Redlands Daily Facts. May 8, 2011
* * *

Issues with Statistics

How to deal with cancer in dogs, which has become a national epidemic (7), is a question for another day. In the meantime, I learned that one challenge in getting the number of dogs and cats euthanized is there is no real accounting done at the national level. Most surveys do not look at all shelters, only some. However, focusing on the issue from the lessons from the PBS movie, (8) support for existing shelters, university coursework and through the media must be part of the reason the kills are down from 3.6 million to 2.1 million. Students that are interested in being a part of getting the number of kills down further should learn about the elements of this great success.

In the meantime, a good start might be to share the success stories of those that contributed to reducing the number of kills from 3.6 to 2.1 million.

* * *

7. Laurie Caplan MSC - Master of Science in Veterinary Medicine. "Causes of Cancer in Dogs." www.helpyourdogfightcancer.com/CausesPrevention.shtml
8. *Shelter Me; Let's Go Home.* PBS

* * *

Table 7:

Reducing Animal Euthanization and Cruelty on Campus

The reduction of dog and cat euthanization from 3.6 million to 2.1 million nationally is a great start, but perhaps New Englanders can do more.

Four Steps in PBS Movie *Shelter Me* **for Classroom Analysis**	1. Put restrictions on breeders. 2. Neuter cats and dogs from shelters. 3. Place the shelters in attractive locations. 4. Support our Shelters! You can donate money or time.
The Role of College Radio and School Newspapers	College radio and newspapers can promote volunteers at no-kill shelters and link campuses to pets in danger of being killed. High school newspapers can play a powerful role; you don't have to be 21 to stick up for abused animals!
The NHES	The National Humane Education Society is a group whose work might be featured in the classroom. You can see their comments on "factory farm" regulation below. **The NHES on Factory Farms:** https://nhes.org/3372-2/
New England Groups that Support Adoption and More	1. Strut Your Mutt. 2. Pets for Veterans. 3. Northeast Animal Shelter (Our largest no-kill shelter). 4. The Animal Rescue League in Boston offers a complete range of services to fight animal cruelty.
The Fifteen Minute Rule & the NHES	This book promotes we try doing fifteen minutes of critical thinking a year on reducing animal suffering, which might be an increase of 14 minutes and 59 seconds. The *National Humane Education Society* is a group whose work is worth of some of that time.

117. How well do New England college newspapers engage with reducing animal cruelty? a Survey of the contributions of New England's seven nationally ranked college papers revealed the results below and on the facing page.

The Harvard Crimson "Confronting Cruelty; Harvard Should Not Tolerate Unnecessary Cruelty in its Labs", published on January 26, 2012, was a strong statement. An article by Natasha Daly in *National Geographic* on February 22, 2017 says *The Crimson* one of five New England papers to "report on patterns of abuse at several private research facilities against dogs and primates".

Tech Online Edition (MIT) No found entries on reducing animal cruelty.

The Brown Daily Herald The article "Mercy for Animals Fellow fights for animal rights", by Kate Talerico, on February 25, 2015, highlights some great work.

The Dartmouth "College Faces Animal Abuse Claims", by Julian Nathan was the best article I found.

The Vermont Cynic The lone article showed a "Not Found Error 404" message.

The Heights I found two outstanding articles; one on helping the disabled and one on the opioid epidemic, (9) but nothing on animal cruelty. One helpful feature of *The Heights* is readers can see all articles ever written by past and present writers on one page, which functions as an accessible database, should future writers focus on animal cruelty.

The Tufts Daily "Circus Decisions Should Prompt Deeper Understanding of Jumbo as a Mascot", March 8, 2015. Lots of discussion of an elephant as their mascot, few details on how to improve their situation. Great paper, but they can do better.

Yale Daily The New Haven, CT student paper distinguishes itself with a wide range of articles on animal rights and many other progressive subjects.

In summary, there is good work being done to prevent unnecessary cruelty by New England schools, but there is also nearly unlimited room for improvement.

Student Newspaper from Pennsylvania State College.
School and college newspapers have a special role to play.

* * *

9. *The Heights*, Marta Seitz Author page. www.bcheights.com/archive.php/author/marta-seitz/
* * *

Rail to Trail programs throughout the country offer great opportunities for better health and pastimes for today's students.

118-130:
How New England College Coursework is Responding to the Needs of Communities

Community colleges provide a demonstrably effective way to educate and train citizens to attain family-sustaining jobs."

- Teresa B. Jones, Associate Professor at Greenfield Community College, Testimony Submitted for Hearing: American Energy Jobs: Opportunities for Education

118. Why is the history of the railroad in New England a subject worthy of being study? Like much of the United States, the social, cultural and architectural landscape of New England has largely evolved around cars. This is particularly true in rural areas and suburbs where most residents are obliged to commute to work or school by car alone. While cars are undeniably time efficient forms of transportation, they are do not provide more active, cost-efficient or eco-friendly lifestyles—all of which are becoming increasingly desirable in our current economic and environmental climate. Children that are able to safely walk to school can reap considerable health benefits; to learn more about that, see the website of *Safe Routes*.

Trains and Old New England
Before the advent of the car a century ago, it was once said that *"one could start at any hour from almost any town in New England and make the journey in an incredibly short time."* (1) This was thanks to the vibrant rail system that developed in New England during the middle of nineteenth century. Over time, however, cars, buses and motorcycles gradually supplanted the role of the railroads. These tracks remained untouched until the recent development of "rail trails," the conversion of old railroad land into multi-use trails for activities such as walking, biking, jogging, and cross-country skiing.

Trains to Rail Trails
The implications of this trend of conversions are far-reaching, because towns with old railroad land have a readily-available resource to convert into walkable green space. This space can make connections to other towns, providing alternative routes to highways and main roads. This doesn't negate the value of pedestrian walkways or bike zones running throughout town and city centers; but are costly compared to the return on investment for rail trails. (2)

* * *

1. Danvers (Ma.) Rail Trail, History
2. The information on the cost of paths and walkways comes from the site of the Pedestrian and Bicycle Information Center, which is funded by the U.S. Department of Transportation Federal Highway Administration (referenced in Chapter Three, Note 4). The PBIC addresses pedestrian and bicycle issues for community planners, engineers and private citizens.

* * *

119. How have attitudes toward vocational education in Massachusetts changed and how has vocational education itself changed? In 1996, when MassINC published their first report The State of the American Dream, one of the main points was the need for more vocational education. At the time, the principles of that report were often received with indifference and snobbery, and I believe that students felt those attitudes. In fact, that report made mention of such pressures, although since then attitudes have changed. Some now emphasize now that there are enough seats for prospective students in plumbing, electricity, carpentry or other areas for students to acquire job skills. Another change is that the number of trades now offered at Massachusetts vocational schools has grown to almost forty.

Combining Traditional and Vocational Studies Another point in the report *The State of the American Dream.* (3) that bears repeating is the option for to implement a combination of traditional and vocational studies. At the time of the report (1996), only seven percent of students were enrolled in vocational programs. According to that report;

"not only would thirty to forty percent of students be better suited for vocational programs, but as many as fifty percent would benefit from doing a combination of the two".

Vocational Education and the Articulation Agreements One important change in Massachusetts vocational education are the Articulation Agreements instituted by Massachusetts Community Colleges. What that and other agreements mean is that students can now continue their vocational education and have some vocational school credit recognized at Massachusetts Community Colleges.

* * *

3. MassINC., "The State of the American Dream". 1996

* * *

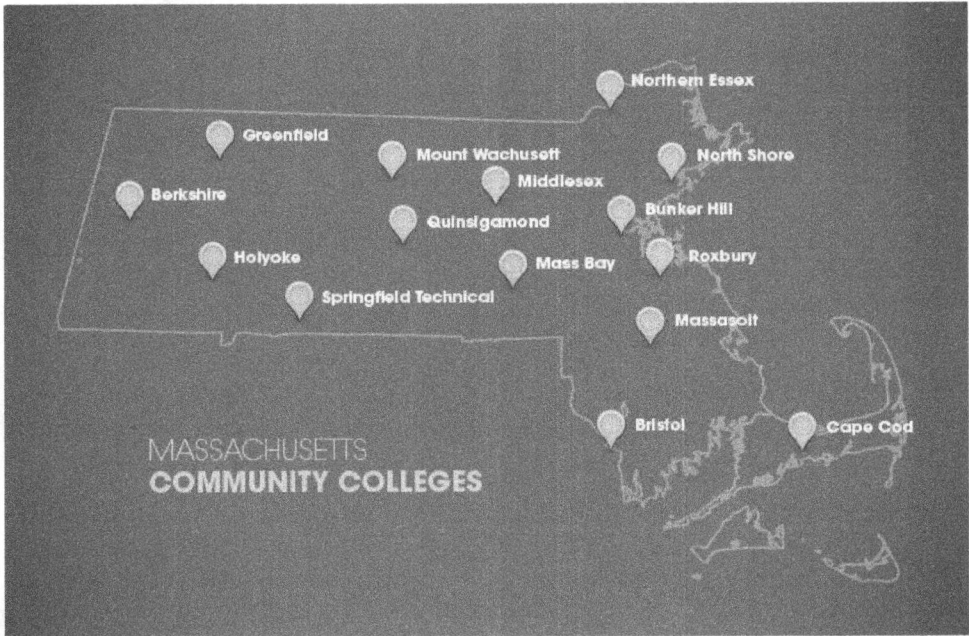

MASSACHUSETTS
COMMUNITY COLLEGES

Community colleges in Massachusetts offer a wide range of programming at an affordable price, and are strategically located in different regions of the state. However, although the focus of this book is support of Massachusetts Community colleges, according to an article by Leon Gorman and John McKernan, the success of the community colleges in Maine is one of the great success stories of the region.

"In 2003, when the state's technical colleges transitioned to community colleges, there were 10,000 students in the system. Today, enrollment has risen 80% to over 18,000 students."

The successes at community colleges in Vermont are also striking. As the President of Vermont Technical College Patricia Moulton said; "*we seek to be the workforce solution for Vermont*". Their story is here *in order to learn what is working.*

120. How can good statistics help us to understand job creation, and with it support agricultural programs? If we hear that new jobs were created, more context is helpful. How many people retired? How many of those jobs are temporary? How much is just coming back from Covid? It was only in The *Boston Herald* that I learned that Massachusetts farms were struggling, with as many as 10%, or 500 closing or in danger. They also did a good video titled "Massachusetts Farmers Fight to Stay Afloat", which was informative. It was then and only then I learned that a full 500 Massachusetts farms were dying, and, quite frankly, that is not acceptable.

* * *

4. Leon Gorman, John McKernan
5. Community College Articulation Agreements
www.masscc.org/technical-high-schools-transfer-agreements/?amp

* * *

Massachusetts Agricultural Employment Stats Example

2021 Mass. Ag Jobs	28,000 full-time positions (actual current)
2022 Mass. Ag Jobs	28,500 (fictional)

One of the best student articles I found on New England farming, which included some good statistics, was titled "Friedman School Screens Forgotten Farms, Discusses New England Dairy Farms", in *The Tufts Daily* on April 13, 2018. One takeaway quote was the following:

"New England has really high land values, high property taxes and high development pressures on the land. There aren't many thriving rural economies in New England."

Sarah Gardner, Enironmental Studies Lecturer, Williams College

One takeaway statistic from that article was that the number of dairy farms in New England has dropped from 20,000 in 1959 to less than 2000 in 2012, with only 117 left in Massachusetts. I understand we need more than just statistics, but sometimes they help. For farm jobs to be an option for New England students, we need to support New England farms. Shopping online, it should be easier to support New England agriculture via delivery and preserve local farms and employment.

See: Mass Grown. www.massrnc/farmlocator/mobilemap.aspx

121. After two years of working with children with extreme emotional and neurological disorders, did I have any brilliant insights worth sharing? No. After working with students at the grammar, middle and high school level for up to six hours a day for two years, one might think I would have a few insights, but I really did not. All I could say is that occupational therapy, or finding out what the students like to do, was the best therapy I saw. However, the quality of a course in Adolescent Psychology I took around 2012, as required for certification, was a gamechanger.

The course was at Salem State, one of the old state teacher's colleges, where the devotion to the craft of teaching is still alive and well. The professor had forty years experience working with young people, and it showed. Every class was engaging and interactive. The piece on "family mapping" changed my thinking on what are often considered broken situations. The biggest takeaway was how even a small change can make a big difference. Anyone who has ever worked hard at anything can tell you about the importance of the "little things".

Teachers, especially new ones trying to find their way, can benefit from having a master teacher as a mentor, to help them work out the big and the little things.

122. What is the state of teaching personal finance in Massachusetts? A 2012 article asked if the push to teach personal finance in the schools was losing steam, but a conversation with a high school educator in Boston was encouraging, and he said they now teach personal finance. (6) However, the hope is that *all students* have the opportunity to learn about mortgages, financing, renting, and credit. Teaching it as part of math class is one option.

At the college level, a one day seminars include Salem State University's financial literacy workshop known as SM.AR.T. Taught by economics faculty the workshop addresses how to make a financial plan, understand credit scores and borrowing, as well as offering core information about banking, saving and investing. The courses were highly popular and packed. In the words of one student;

"I instantly fell in love with the idea because I consider it very important. In college, we learn the basics of math and history but when it comes down to the nitty-gritty stuff of wanting to function in the job, you need to learn that too."

This free program is rare; it was only the second of its kind at a Massachusetts public college or university. (7) However, as was revealed through an informative interview and exchange of emails with a SSU professor in 2016, the SM.AR.T. program is just one way they are teaching personal finance. See questions 155 to 157 for more on this.

123. How is education responding to the issue of affordable housing in Massachusetts? Programs like those at Salem State University are helping to assure that young people have the basic knowledge of personal finance they need to eventually make good real estate decisions. The SM.AR.T. program highlighted above is only one of the effective approaches to this. Throughout my years of teaching high school, I was struck by how few of my students had *any understanding* of mortgages or how they worked. As a graduate student, I was surprised that most college students did not understand this stuff either. After the housing crash in 2008 left many millions owing lenders more than their homes were worth, teaching young people about mortgages and finance should be a priority.

124. How is education responding to issues in transportation? The coursework provided by the Pedestrian, Bike and Information Center is, in my opinion, the number answer to the desire for more walking and biking options. According to The Surface Transportation Policy's Project report *Transportation Costs and the American Dream*, transportation costs make up 19 percent of American household budgets. (8) So, finding affordable, and healthy modes of transportation while mediating the high fuel cost of driving is important.

* * *

6. Ethan Geiling, "Is Financial Education in the Schools in Decline?" CFED, April 4, 2012. www.cfed.org/

7. Laidler, "Free Finance Class a Hit at Salem State". The Boston Globe

8. "Transportation Costs and the American Dream", Reason Foundation, September 1, 2003. www.reason.org/

9. Polly Nichol, "Shared Housing Takes Many Forms," Vermont Housing & Conservation Board, accessed May 5, 2012. www.vhcb.org/

* * *

PBIC Coursework Many of us would enjoy walking and bike paths to give people healthy options for getting around, but how do we do so? The number one rule is to create "local experts" that have done the coursework prescribed by the Pedestrian, Bike and Information Center. The challenge is that, within New England, the *Harvard School of Public Health* is the only school to offer the course on the budgeting, political and engineering aspects of building a long-term plan to be bike and walking friendly.

See: *pedbikeinfo.org*

Safe Routes The *Safe Routes* walk-to-school programs and stories are another dimension of this, as outlined in question 121. However, the best way to learn about the organization it to go to their website.

See: *saferoutesinfo.org*

Progressive University Coursework This book advocates all the steps outlined in a previous chapter with regard to going green at universities. You can check out Table 5 on page 52 for more steps to create healthy options in transportation.

125. What is a dimension of personal finance that some New Englanders might benefit from? A course that addressed the many legal complications of shared ownership might be of great use to those looking to downsize, adjuncts, veterans with PTSD and others. Shared ownership can mean paying a portion of a mortgage rather than rent, splitting other costs and building capital rather than going into debt. However, most Massachusetts mortgage brokers I spoke to about co-ownership had never even heard of such arrangements.

On April 11th, 2018 I opened *The Boston Herald* and saw an article titled "Disabled house mates take pride in home ownership". It was the first time I had ever seen an article on this subject. The reprint of the *Chicago Tribune* article told the story of three older, disabled men that bought a home together. As a result of supporting each other emotionally and keeping costs low, they seemed quite content. They were able to get their mortgage through an Illinois Housing Development program called *Project Ground Floor,* although according to the article, "such arrangements are still a rarity". Another perspective on shared housing is the following;

"Shared housing provides a creative solution for people who, for a variety of reasons, choose to live in a mutually supportive environment. It is an alternative housing arrangement for many rural Vermonters who do not have access to affordable housing in their towns or who could not remain independent without a supportive environment." (9)

For this to even possibly work, though, lawyers need to research and develop models of shared ownership contracts *that address every contingency*. (10)

* * *

9. Polly Nichol, "Shared Housing Takes Many Forms," Vermont Housing & Conservation Board, accessed May 5, 2012. www.vhcb.org/
10. Chicago Tribune Project Ground Floor "Disabled house mates take pride in home ownership"
* * *

126. What is the future of shared space markets in a New England? The Boston Public Market is unique and worthy of study because it involves 35 business renting a high traffic common space to sell their food products. Perhaps COVID-19 has likely put a damper on so such markets, as they involve so many people in such tight spaces, but this is certainly a business model worth learning about. In the meantime, you can check out their website to see the layout and wide variety of unique options under one roof.

127. What is one school contributing to shared space food markets? Pennsylvania State. Trips to New England towns are fun now because industry is in the air; the increased number of shared space markets mean opportunity, but not if someone gets food poisoning. Colleges can help make these stories a reality by offering coursework on food safety, as Pennsylvania State does.

See: www.extension.psu.edu/farmers-market-food-safety

128. What is one existing model of coursework on Social Security that can contribute to elder health and family security? One course at the University of Texas that teaches students how to maximize Social Security by looking at the 82 different pathways to enrolling in the federal program. (11) It would be interesting to know if similar courses in New England exist; I have yet to find one.

Young People Can Handle This Tip O'Neill contributed enormous amounts to Massachusetts because he started young. Running for office as a senior at Boston College in 1936, he began advocating for the programs elders needed most, including Social Security. Whether students choose to take such a course to begin planning for retirement for themselves or to assist a family member in their choice, this is the kind of practical coursework young people need.

Some Young People are Forced to Handle This I knew one college freshman who was the highest functioning adult in her family, and she's not alone. A course on Social Security like this could allow her to help older adults in the family to make the best possible choice in this critical area. In this one student's case, she was forced to not only be the peacemaker, but both work and go to school full-time.

129. Why is the standard for New England professors to use their own books in their classes? I think it's greeat that adjunct and tenured professors write books that add value to fields of study or to communities. I for one challenge the idea that they shouldn't use their books in their classes. From running a small publishing house, I know there are books that have yet to be written that the the public could benefit from. An article in *The Collegiate* that stated that professors who assign their own books to their own classes are "egomaniacs", and another article suggested that professors are profiting too much. The best response to that was one article that outlined the standards for such a choice. See: How "Professors Can Assign their own books with a clear conscience".

* * *

11. "Maximizing Social Security", University of Texas Extension School.

* * *

130. What is the role of veterans in boosting enrollment at New England colleges and with it the New England economy? Not only are there many veterans in New England that could benefit from a good job, but one million veterans will be coming home from overseas over the next decade, which is about 40,000 in New England, and they may represent the best new source of students for New England colleges. As one veteran said the video "A Future for Veterans in Manufacturing", (mfgInstitute) "someone who has received an honorable discharge is certainly someone who has accomplished something. the video "Women Veterans: Military to Manufacturing", posted by Arconic, points out how female veterans seeking employment and American manufacturing needs might converge. See pages 120 to 131 for a more complete look at the needs and potential contributions of veterans.

131. Why is the timebanking system so powerful and what is its role in the schools? For starters, I don't see it as my role to say what should be or not be taught; I only provide this book as a guide for parents, students and educators. To fulfill my role as a writer and best serve those three groups, I need to share what I have learned, as that knowledge is largely unknown. To do so, I will use lots of short sentences in a short column to compart lots of applicable information.

Short Sentences 1

Timebanking is like barter, except barter is between two people. In a timebank you give your time, but can take back "time dollars" from anyone in the group. Getting a time bank going requires a lot of work and patience. One person can't get it started alone; you need need one primary coordinator and five board members. The PC and board members should expect to do 10-15 hours a week work for a year. It's important to offer what you enjoy, not your profession.

Short Sentences 2

Timebanks are about healthy, symbiotic relationships of trust. People not interested in that will lose interest and drop out. It's important to insist that people "log in " their hours so the coordinators can keep track of exchanges. Some colleges have timebanks, most don't. Right now, less than 0.01% of the population participates in timebanking, although I think a reasonable goal for the future is 2% participation.

Short Sentences on the Elderly and Timebanks

For older or isolated people, 5-10 hours doing what they enjoy for others can be a huge boost. The Rushey Green TB in England is the best example I know of of a timebank helping older people.

Table 8:

Schools Engaging with New England Communities

Every faculty member and school leader should arrive at work with confidence and certainty about their school and viability of their future. Or so one might hope. But that is not the case for as many as half of New England colleges, according to an article in Forbes by Richard Vedder. On the other hand, manufacturers and other companies have difficulty finding workers. And, many veterans are on their way home in the next decade: 40,000 to New England and 1,000,000 nationwide.

Challenges Many Colleges Face Nationally	1. Declining Enrollment (Byrne, Mary *Wicked Local Danvers*) 2. Decreasing Revenues (Vedder, Richard. *Forbes*) 3. Colleges Closing Doors (America's Lost Colleges) 4. Retention Rates Many enroll in community colleges but retention rates tell the full story. (www.mass.edu) 5. Smaller Applicant Pool. (Vedder, Richard) 6. Many students say they would rather work and make money. (Byrne, Mary) 7. Many college graduates struggle to find work. (Weber, Korn) 8. Competition for federal funding.
All Book Tables	Table 1: Core Points in Education - page 13 Table 2: Quality of Life for Adjuncts - page 32 Table 3. Levels of Student Language Ability - page 38 Table 4: Language Departments Adapt - page 49 Table 5: Existing Measures of Green Colleges - page 52 Table 6: Dimensions of State and National Park Creation Table 7: Reducing Animal Euthanization and Cruelty - page 68 Table 8: Schools Engaging with NE Communities - page 79 Table 9: Restoring the New England Middle Class - page 86 Table 10: Innovation at New England Colleges - page 93 Table 11: New England Farm Models for Study - page 97 Table 12: Support the Disabled, Support the Economy - page 101 Table 13: Understanding Unemployment Rating Systems - pg.102 Table 14: The Frustrated Mom's 12 Pack - page 106 Table 15: On Campus Support of Manufacturing - page 110 Table 16: On Campus Support of Veterans - page 141
New Market: Veterans and Adults	Many veterans in New England could use work. With one million veterans coming home nationwide in the next ten years, with about 40,000 in New England, we need to be ready. Two videos to understand their situation are: "A Future for Veterans in Manufacturing" and "Women Veterans: Military to Manufacturing."

How can students in Maine help lead the conversation between opposing parties to create new conservation projects?

Table 9:
Restoring the New England Middle Class

"We seek to be the workforce and education solution for Vermont."

- Patricia Moulton, President of Vermont Technical College

132. What is an example of a complete approach to job creation by a regional college? The work being done at Vermont Technical College is an approach to workforce development that needs to be made common knowledge among educators, which is the reason it is here. In an interview with WAMC, Northeast Television, Vermont Technical College President Patricia Moulton said; "We seek to be the workforce and education solution for Vermont." That's a strong statement, and after studying the website and speaking to an administrator for the college, I believe we need to emphasize two benefits to the public; the direct benefits of VTC programs to students and also the value that the study and perhaps imitation of these programs can bring to other parts of New England.

The VTC Model The apprenticeship program is a system by which students do 8,000 hours of work under a mentor while doing 144 hours of classroom work. The role of VTC in this is twofold; they help to create that connection and assure the employer with the fact that their apprentice is getting the classroom training they need. Just recently, VTC went from a 96% placement rate for graduates to 100%. Additionally, they have both two and four year programs while offering training in advanced manufacturing and other fields. (1)

133. What is the role of New England colleges and universities in building up manufacturing and quality manufacturing jobs? Colleges and universities are the key to our success in creating manufacturing jobs, because the biggest issue we have in manufacturing is a skilled workforce. Relevant to the efforts of educators to bring back manufacturing are a few steps, featured below.

Flagship University Manufacturing The University of Maine, the University of New Hampshire and the University of Connecticut. Each of the manufacturer training operations at those colleges has a slightly different focus, and readers interested in opportunities in manufacturing may want to learn about them.

Industry Partnerships Cooperation between industries such as that between York County Community College and Pratt- Whitney mean that the community college is tasked with training workers for a specific need in industry. As for the marketing of these industry partnerships, the information a little harder to find; I only knew about the partnership between York County Community college and Pratt Whitney because I went to the college website and also had the opportunity to talk to the president of the college.

* * *

1. www.vtc.edu/news/vermont-tech-class-2016-reports-100-placement-rate

* * *

Massachusetts Manufacturing Extension Partnership Training Models

Collaboration between the Massachusetts Manufacturing Partnership and a few colleges have created programs to get workers ready for manufacturing jobs in as little as seven to eight weeks. In Edwin L. Aguirre's 2015 article on the web page of the University of Massachusetts Lowell titled "MassMEP, UMass Lowell Unveil New Workforce Training Programs", it becomes clear that such a program is addressing a critical shortfall in skilled workers. The partnerships between the different New England MEPs and New England colleges.

"The manufacturing industry in Massachusetts is facing a critical shortfall in skilled workers, with jobs currently unfilled and more expected to open up over the next ten years". (2)

One fact to be aware of is that, according to a Mass MEP rep I spoke with, Worcester Polytechnic Institute and the University of Massachusetts at Lowell are the only Massachusetts schools that have the facilities to support the eight week MEP Trainings.

134. What are trends affecting colleges nationally and what are some efforts to boost enrollment at the community college nearest you? As has already been stated on page 79, issues affecting colleges nationally include: 1) declining enrollment, 2) decreasing revenues, 3) colleges closing doors, 4) low retention rates, 5) a smaller applicant pool, 6) potential students expressing that they would rather work, 7) graduates struggling to find work, and 8) rising federal interest payments. The source articles for trends 1-7 are on page 79. As for rising federal interest payments, the numbers below are from the Congressional Budget Office Report "An Update to the Budget Outlook: 2023-2033".

Projected Net Federal Interest Payments

2020 $345 Billion
2025 $773 Billion
2030 $1.165 trillion
2033 $1.44 trillion

According to an article in the *Danvers Wicked Local* website, enrollment at Massachusetts community colleges has dropped from 64,964 students in 2011 to 58,569 in 2016. (3) The article stated that for Massachusetts students, a fear of student debt was combined with the fact that "*students would rather go into the workforce have contributed to the problem*". For that reason, the following shares a bit about what is working.

Existing Successes

A. Industry Partnerships Collaboration between local industry and community colleges creates jobs. One example is the partnership between York County CC and Pratt-Whitney in Maine, whereby students are trained specifically to work for Pratt Whitney. (4)

B. Apprenticeships See the list of existing apprenticeships at New England Community Colleges on page 89.

* * *

2. "Mass MEP, UMass Lowell Unveil New Workforce Training Program", University of Massachusetts at Lowell. www.uml.edu

3. Mary Byrne, "North Shore Community College Pilots Free College Program". Wicked Local Danvers. April 20, 2017. danvers.wickedlocal.com

4. John Laidler, "Free Finance Class a Hit at Salem State." Boston.com, March 3, 2011. www.boston.com/

* * *

C. Manufacturing Support According to the video interview "Shop Talk" by the *Worcester Business Journal,* (5) Quinsigamond Community College has done an outstanding job of providing skilled workers for local manufacturers.

D. Preparation for STEM Jobs Massachusetts Bay Community College now offers a comprehensive STEM program. See: pages 114-118 for the section on STEM.

E. The Role of the National Junior College Athletic Association One thing that attracts is sports, and the positive role of the NJCAA is something that more might learn about. For the record, I watched the Division 1 NJCAA football championship on TV in December of 2023, and it was a blast. It just felt like pure sport, and the all-natural joy of the winning team in the sparsely attended stadium is something I will not soon forget. Within New England, community colleges participate in Division 3 sports as part of Region 21, or XXI.

F. Maine and Vermont Community Colleges While community colleges throughout New England struggle with the eight trends described in question 134, community college enrollment in Maine has gone from 10,000 to 18,000. This may be because of the highly practical programming. (6)

135. How is the decline in enrollment statewide in line with North Shore Community College? One of the sharper declines in enrollment is happening at North Shore Community college, which went from 5,431 students in 2011 to 4.283 students in 2016. (8) NSCC responded with the "Promise Award", a free college program designed to boost enrollment numbers. However, it seems the enrollment decline was caused by many factors outside our control, including the eight factors on the facing page.

136. Which New England journalists are good sources for articles on education? The article by Derrick Z. Jackson on the wish list list of community college presidents was very helpful, as were other articles by the Globe writer. Laura Krantz, also of the *Boston Globe,* has a wide range of articles on subjects in education, including mental health. You can see all of her articles on muckrack.com.

137. How can student newspapers contribute to conversations on the subject of job creation? As NPR put it; *"truly good journalism is a craft, not just a blog post. Seeing something close up, but also reporting it with perspective....if school newspapers begin to disappear, I hope there are other ways for students to learn that."* (9) As the intensity of the competition for federal money increases, as foretold by the numbers on page 82 under "Projected Net Federal Interest Payments", those looking for funding will need effective advocates, and maybe school newspapers will play a role in that.

* * *

5. Youtube Video: "Shop Talk" with Jack Healy. *Worcester Business Journal.*

6. MassINC "The State of the American Dream" 1996.

7. The website of Massachusetts Bay Community College is one Massachusetts institution with a very elaborate and well organized web page for STEM. SEE: STEM - Science, Technology, Engineering and Mathematics. www.massbay.stem

8. Mary Byrne, "North Shore Community College Pilots Free College Program". *Wicked Local Danvers.* April 20, 2017.

9. Scott Simon "High School Newspapers: An Endangered Species". npr.org June 1, 2013

* * *

138. What are some existing successes by new authors that contribute to the local economy? Authors that broach new subjects add value to the communities they live or work in. From association with the *Salem House Press* and researching for this book, it became clear that there are thousands of books on niche subjects the public can benefit from. Books with even a relatively small circulation, be it 100-150 copies a year, can make a significant positive impact in specialized areas.

Safety: One university president wrote a book about safe spaces entitled *Safe Enough Spaces. (Yale University Press. 2019)* There may be few things as irritating to an author as a critic critiquing a book he has never read, but one thing is for sure: being safe never goes out of style.

Conservation: A Meeting of Land and Sea One existing example is *A Meeting of Land and Sea; Nature and the Future of Martha's Vineyard,* written as both history and as a model of conservation for New England.

Language Learning Good foreign language easy readers are sometimes hard to find, although companies like Blaine Ray produces easy readers that are accessible to a wide range of levels.

Local History When the grandmother in the movie *The Economics of Happiness* said "local history is knowledge of life, and we need to make sure that local knowledge never dies", she was advocating for the idea of "grandmother's colleges". However, that was also a great plug for the value of preserving local history.

139. What is an attitude shift that needs to happen for professors? In an article in *The Chronicle of Higher Education,* called "How These Professors Assign Their Own Books With a Clean Conscience", the subject of professors assigning their own books was discussed at length. One conclusion was that "the professor should negotiate with a publisher to eliminate royalties for any book purchased at the professor's institution while agreeing to take lower royalties overall". Another article in *Collegiate Times,* a student took concerned himself with the fact that the professor might make (gasp) $1,350 over the course of the semester in book sales, assuming he or she taught four courses. A better attitude might be to embrace professors and their books, and assess what contribution they make.

140. What is a recent development that adds value to vocational high school? The establishment of the articulation agreements in 2011 added value to vocational education because they mean that accomplishments in vocational school are recognized. This step builds on the conclusion of MassINC. in their 1996 publication *The State of the American Dream,* which stated that there need to be enough seats in the vocational schools to meet demand. At the time in Massachusetts, only seven percent of students attended vocational schools, although in the opinion of MassINC., this number should be 30-40%, with as many as 50% of students doing a combination of traditional and vocational learning. (10)

* * *

10. MassINC "The State of the American Dream" 1996.

* * *

The Role of the Articulation Agreements

The various articulation agreements help those who acquired a skiil or skills at a technical high school get credit for and choose a program of study at the right Community College. As community colleges struggle to stay afloat, more public awareness of these agreements support a pool of engaged applicants for the time to come. In 2011, fifteen Massachusetts Community Colleges and Chapter 74 approved secondary career/vocational technical high schools established agreements in 14 fields. (11)

Articulation Agreement Courses Accepted:
1. Drafting
2. Hospitality Management
3. Manufacturing/Engineering
4. Business Technology
5. Culinary Arts
6. Health Assisting (CNA)
7. Transportation
8. Medical Assisting
9. Arts & Communication
10. Carpentry
11. Information Technology
12. HVAC
13. Early Childhood Education
14. Machine Tool Technology

141. How do sports and the articulation agreements boost the outlook of Massachusetts community college students, and what recent experience influenced the creation of this question? The articulation agreements mean that students are continuing their work from high school. Sports help students to stay in shape, feel more comfortable and be part of a team in their new learning environment. During 2007 and 2008 I worked at a large high school where about half of students were not going to college, but also did not have a job lined up. Honestly, I was struck by that, and that experience played a role in the creation of this question.

You can check out the conference in which many Massachusetts community colleges compete: that of the National Junior College Athletic Association Region 21, or NJCAA Region 21.

See: Region XXI Composite Schedule www.njcaaregionxxi.com

* * *

11. Massachusetts Community Colleges Articulation Agreements.
www.masscc.org/technical-high-schools-transfer-agreements/?amp
* * *

Table 9:
Restoring the New England Middle Class

The overarching goal of this table is to demonstrate how community colleges are creating careers and new industries, while also being mindful of changes on the horizon.

Community College Value	1. With the 2011 Articulation Agreements, vocational school graduates receive certificates for skills acquired, and in turn community college credit. See page 85 for the list of accepted skills.
	2. Systems such as Mass Transfer and NH Transfer facilitate easy transfer of credits from community to state, flagship and private colleges.
	3. Community colleges are relatively affordable, and their websites are easy to navigate to check out programs and prices.
	4. Community colleges are great places for pilot programs.
Community College Job Creation Models of Success	1. *Manufacturing* Quinsigamond Community College trains the workers that NE manufacturers desperately need.
	2. *Apprenticeships* As Vermont Technical College and other community colleges offer apprenticeships. See page 89.
	3. *Industry Partnerships* between community colleges and companies fuel regional economic growth. Example: York County Community College and Parattt-Whitney Program.
	4. York County Community College offers industry partnerships and apprenticeships that may explain why enrollment at Maine community colleges increased from 10,000 to 18,000.
	5. *Farm Jobs* Agricultural programs at Greenfield CC and others fuel the growth of agriculture (See Table 11).
	6. *STEM Training* STEM coursework can be done at CCs. See the Massachusetts Bay College STEM program.
Sports & Radio	1. *Sports* Athletes develop in community college conferences under the umbrella of the National Junior College Athletic Association, or NJCAA.
	2. *Radio Stations* such as WCCH 105.3 at Springfield Technical College offer a chance to build broadcasting skills.
Sustainability: Top Two Concerns	1. Federal Interest Payments are scheduled to rise from $345 billion in 2020 to $1.165 trillion in 2030, and to unsustainable levels after. See: "Rising Federal Interest Payments" on page 82.
	2. Social Security: See: Social Security "Long-term Financial Outlook" on the website of the Social Security Administration.

142 to 150:
New England Education and Local Economies

"Over the next decade, nearly 3.5 million manufacturing jobs will likely need to be filled, and the skills gap is expected to result in 2 million of those jobs going unfilled."

Jacqueline Moloney, President of University of Massachusetts Lowell

142. What might the role of colleges and universities in Massachusetts be in building walking and bike infrastructure? A good start would be for more New England Colleges to offer the Pedestrian, Bike and Information Center coursework, (PBIC) coursework, because to my knowledge the Harvard School of Public Health is the only New England institution that has offered the coursework. For colleges looking to become relevant in the realm of green infrastructure, offering this coursework is one way. A PBIC coursework syllabus can be found online.

143. What is the role of charter schools in Massachusetts and why is innovation so important? "Charter schools are "a publicly funded independent school established by teachers, parents, or community groups under the terms of a charter with a local or national authority."(1) The first Massachusetts charter school opened in 1995 and as of June of 2016, 71 charter schools were educating more than 32,000 Massachusetts students (about 3 percent of the total).(2) In Massachusetts, charter schools receive state funding normally allotted to the mainstream DOE budget, which is why they are so controversial. As an article in the *Boston Globe* said; "if you want to understand the charter school debate, follow the money." (3)

Understanding that *Boston Globe* article is a good start to understanding the charter school debate, but one fact not emphasized enough in this article was the key role that innovation is supposed to play in charter schools. In fact, it was only from watching the show *Basic Black* on PBS that I learned that innovation is required of charter schools in order to get funding. I also inferred from the tone of that show that it was questionable how much innovation was in fact taking place.

In hindsight, I'm not at all surprised that *Basic Black* alerted me to the issue of innovation in charter schools, as that show spent a lot of time talking about poverty and education in Boston in a way I did not hear discussed elsewhere in 2013. (4)

* * *

1. Definition of Charter School from Google Definitions
2. Perez, Felix, "MA School Board Chairman, Under Fire, Donates $100K to Charter School Campaign", *Education Votes,* September 20, 2016 http://educationvotes.nea.org
3. Levenson, Michael, "Money is at the Heart of the Mass. Charter Debate". *The Boston Globe.* April 2, 2016
4. http://saveourpublicschoolsma.com

* * *

Innovation in the Language Classroom

Having taught and studied language classes for many years in many different kinds of schools, I'm keenly aware of the need for innovation in the language classroom, which is the reason for questions 47-85. So, in the event that any charter school decided to focus on teaching languages well, there are plenty of ideas and information here for them to do so.

One of the focuses of the questions in that section is one exchanges, and about how one Italian department does live classes with classes in Italy. An innovative charter school could do more collaboration like this between classes in North and South America. Classes learning Spanish could connect with classes in Latin America or Spain learning English. They can also do individual sessions via Skype, which is a concept that was explored in regards to the Tandem Plus program at the University of Minnesota (5).

144. What is the best website for information on current prices for New England public colleges? The Data Center of the Massachusetts Department of Education. (6) I say that because I have found conflicting and faulty information on many different websites, which of course creates confusion. I would also recommend going to the official pages of other state colleges in the region.

145. What should Massachusetts know about the New England public college system? First, they should know there are affordable options for college in every region of each state.

Cost Students can utilize *The College and Career Readiness Program* model, thus combining lower cost with an effective approach to helping college students plan for paying for their education.

Three Tiered versus Two Tiered System The Massachusetts university system consists of three main parts; the branches of the community colleges, the state colleges and the "flagship" UMass with the multiple branches. There is the same three tiered system other New England states, except for Maine, which has a two tiered system.

Parents should also obviously be aware of cost and programming, but also credit transfer systems and the articulation agreements.

Credit Transfer Systems In Massachusetts, transfers occur through the MassTransfer website, and in New Hampshire through NHTransfer. Each of the other New England states have their own version of this.

Articulation Agreements These determine if students can get credit for work done at a vocational school. What's important to know is that much of the credits received at a community college can be transferred to four year schools.

* * *

5. Tandem Plus, University of Minnesota. https://tandem.unm.edu
6. Data Center of the Massachusetts Department of Education

* * *

Additionally, many community colleges throughout New England now offer college credit for certificates received in vocational schools. By going to the Massachusetts Community College website, you can comfortably surf the sites of all of the fifteen members of the MCC network.

Reducing Student Debt As we look at ways to reduce student debt, we shouldn't overlook the most obvious option; keeping the price of education down. However, the good news is that there are many affordable colleges in New England. I mention tuition alone without tuition and not housing, because in some cases the cost of housing is more than that of tuition.(7) I choose the programs below as examples because they are located in different regions of the New England.

Note: For current prices, see the Data Center on the Mass education website. (8)

Some Existing New England Apprenticeships

Industrial Maintenance Apprenticeship at Vermont Technical College

Electrician Apprenticeship Training at the Community College of Rhode Island

Plumbing Apprenticeship Program at the Community College of Rhode Island

Pre Apprentice Construction Methods and Materials at Roxbury Community College

Manufacturing Apprenticeships at Vermont Technical College

Facilities Maintenance Technician Apprenticeship through Boston Mayor's Office

Railroad Street Youth Project Entrepreneurial Apprenticeship at Berkshire CC

Electrician D Licence at Massasoit Community College

York County Community College Plumbing Apprenticeship

Vermont Technical College Electrical Program

Advanced Manufacturing at the Community College System of New Hampshire, partnered with Apprenticeship NH

Financial Services Apprenticeship at Capital Community College (CT)

Culinary Apprenticeship at Southern Maine CC and Central Maine CC

All Trades by The Connecticut Department of Labor offers a wide variety of apprenticeships, which might be compared to those at community colleges.

* * *

7. Reducing Student Debt
8. "Current Tuition" www.mass.edu/datacenter/tuition/appendixtuitionfeesweight7.asp

* * *

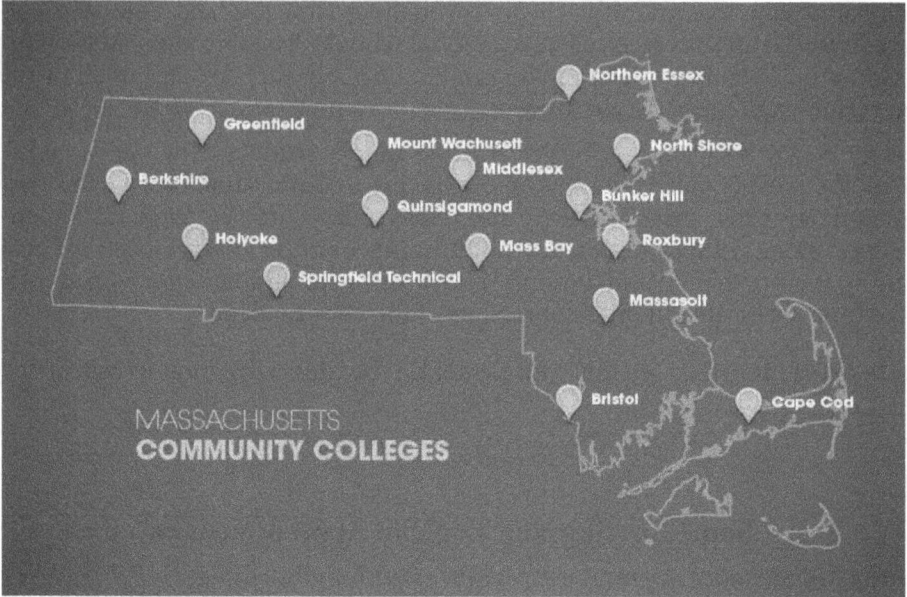

MASSACHUSETTS COMMUNITY COLLEGES

Exercise 1: Checking Prices

Many know there are four year colleges in Massachusetts (page 91) with a tuition not too far north of $10,000, although this is not including housing, which can more than tuition. The official tuition numbers are often deceptive, because they do not include fees. (9) One good exercise is to see what credits can be acquired at the community colleges and then transferred to the state colleges in the six states, which is explained on pages xiii-xiv.

Some Affordable College Options by State

State	College
Vermont	Johnson St., Lyndon St. Castleton St.
New Hampshire	Keene St, Plymouth St.
Maine	University of Maine branches
Massachusetts	See map on page 91
Connecticut	see CT.edu
Rhode Island	Rhode Island College

Exercise 2: Transferring Credits by Major

Transferring credits for your major is often more complicated than transferring credits for college to college. Perhaps this is because individual departments want to maintain standards. However, before students go and get 12 credits for their major and then find out they don't transfer to their favorite college, they might want to look into this.

* * *

9. "Tuition and Mandatory Fees at Massachusetts Public Colleges and Universities". www.mass.edu

* * *

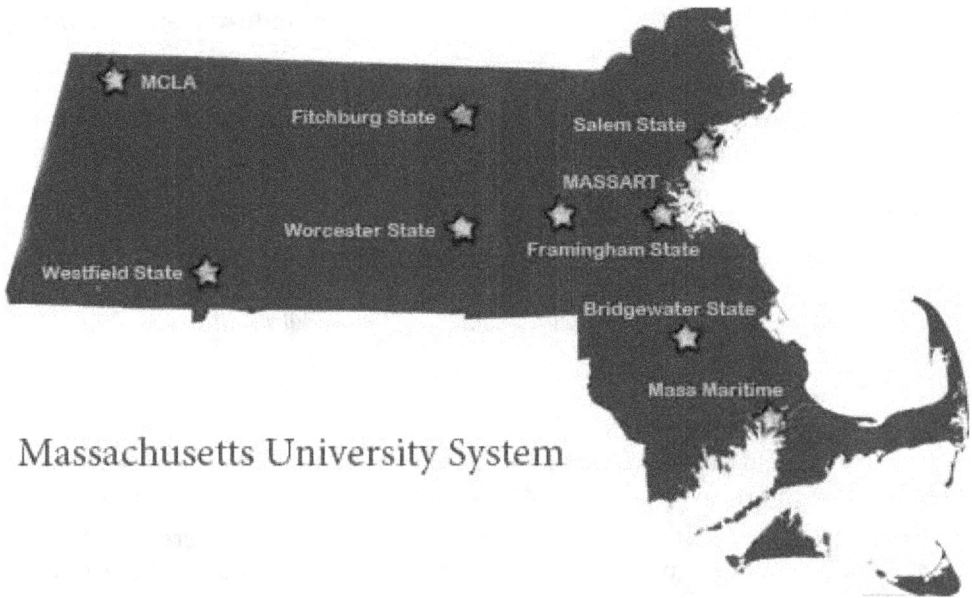

Massachusetts University System

Exercise 3 for Prospective Students

The third and potentially trickiest exercise is for students in high school vocational programs to explore how certificates acquired in vocational school can be transferred to community colleges via the Articulation Agreements. See page 86 for more about this.

Exercise 4: Transferring CC Credit to State Colleges

Another point for parents to know about is that some of community college credits can be transferred to the state or flagship colleges. The previous page shows the map of two year schools in Massachusetts. Also, thanks to new, updated websites, researching the details of all of some of the programs above can smoothly and effectively with a smart phone or computer.

Language Learning and the Affordable Colleges

It is my professional opinion that all of the principles of language learning in questions 47-85 can be applied to any school. The reality is that the most rigorous language programs are most likely to be at the expensive, elite colleges, but any of the affordable colleges that truly committed to making their language programs great, can.

Conservation Biology and Species Extinction

The core principle of innovation on campus should also be applied to conservation biology. As was pointed out by L. Moyer-Horner in her paper; *"Education as a tool for addressing the extinction crisis: moving students from understanding to action"*, students in colleges are being taught about species extinction, but not being given the tools to combat it. As I see it, any college anywhere in New England with students with great passion could do the planet a great service by changing the culture on this.

146. What is one example of a partnership between industry and a university that we need to be aware of? The partnership between the University of Massachusetts at Lowell and the Mass Manufacturing Extension Partnership. The MEP/UMass Lowell program is an eight week, 280 hour program that focuses on developing the worker's CNC (Computer Numerical Control) skills, but also has a broader application in other manufacturing enterprises. As UMass Lowell Chancellor Jacqueline Moloney said;

"The manufacturing industry is facing a critical shortfall in skilled workers, with jobs currently unfilled and more expected top open up within the next ten years.... over the next decade, nearly 3.5 million manufacturing jobs will likely need to be filled, and the skills gap is expected to result in 2 million of those jobs going unfilled."

What's astonishing is the fact that it is stated that "the skills gap is expected to result in 2 million of those jobs being filled". The tone of that statement almost suggests that we would casually accept a loss of 2 million jobs. I have to say that again; I can't believe that we would consider allowing a loss of two million jobs to occur.

This partnership with UMass Lowell is not the only of its kind; there are seven to eight week courses designed to train workers for manufacturing, on the websites of the various state MEPs within New England. Maybe part of the problem in not finding more workers for these programs is marketing. After all, how many people go to the websites of manufacturing extension partnerships?

New England Jobs

We need to be asking ourselves how many of these new partnerships we need in order to address the anticipate shortage of workers. Massachusetts is statistically very convenient because the population is almost exactly one fiftieth of the country. What that means here is that if it's said that two million skilled jobs may go unfilled, then the number for Massachusetts is about one fiftieth of that, or forty thousand. If we include the rest of New England, or another six million residents, that would mean that we're in danger of losing about 80,000 jobs.

MEP Case Studies

As we figure out answers to the two million job question, the many case studies on the website of the MEPs the six New England states can help site visitors learn more about some New England success stories in manufacturing.

Boston College Responds

The decision of Boston College to add a school of Engineering might be seen as one response to the quote of Chancellor Moloney. Or, perhaps it was a response to the article and chart of Steve Lohr, whose contribution to the thinking on STEM and STEM employment is highlighted on page one hundred and sixteen. (10)

* * *

10. Lohr, S. (2017, November 1). Where the STEM Jobs Are (and Where They Aren't). The New York Times. Retrieved from https://mobile.nytimes.com/2017/11/01/education/edlife/stem-jobs-industry-careers.html

* * *

Table 10:
Present and Future of Innovation at New England Colleges

You can be anywhere in New England and be less than two hours from an affordable state college. All of these colleges have pockets of excellence often rooted in their history, but below are some new, lesser known innovations.

Practical Programming	1. The Salem State and Bridgewater St. programs are the Gold Standard for teaching personal finance. (See questions 155-157) 2. Through MassTransfer, NH Transfer and other systems for each state, students can seamlessly transfer credits. 3. Because of a variety of articulation agreements, students receive credit for certificates earned at vocational schools at community colleges, which in turn can transfer to four year schools. 4. Students can utilize *The College and Career Readiness Program* model, thus combining lower cost with an effective approach to helping college students plan for paying for their education.
Johnson State & Climate Change	The unique programming of the affordable Vermont college in the mountains is a model to learn from. *"Students take on the challenges of a growing population, limited energy and climate change while taking courses in six different sciences"*
Creating Skilled Workers	1. Public Colleges are helping to create the skilled workers of the future while supporting manufacturers. (See Table 15 on page 110) 2. Apprenticeship Programs such as those at York County Community College (ME) & Vermont Tech boast high placement rates.
Steve Lohr on STEM	Steve Lohr's groundbreaking chart on STEM education and STEM employment in his N.Y. Times article can effectively inform policy for schools with STEM programming. Lohr, S. (2017, November 1). Where the STEM Jobs Are (and Where They Aren't). *The New York Times.*
Support the Disabled, Support the Economy	Researching ways to develop opportunities for the disabled for this book made it clear that we haven't even scratched the surface of ways to create opportunities for the disabled. See pages 97-101.

147. Why is it important to support the growth of New England agriculture?
Everyone wins when farms are doing well, especially those that are having a hard time. Agricultural programs are unique in that, everyone consumes their products - - food . We all eat. A 2019 *Boston Herald* video "Massachusetts Farms Struggle to Stay Afloat" (Ottolini. 2019) stated that 500 Massachusetts farms were in danger of going out of business. Some older farmers in that video also shared that their children and even grandchildren had left the farm or had little interest in farming.

How Many Farms are There in Massachusetts? According to the Massachusetts Office of Energy and Environmental affairs, there are 28,000 Massachusetts residents on 7,755 farms employed in farming. In New Hampshire, by definition, a farm is a place that sells one thousand dollars of agricultural products a year. So, the potential loss of 500 farms described by Ms. Ottolini in her Herald multi-media piece would be very significant, but to truly understand the impact on food security and the agricultural sector, we need to know more, (11) which is the reason for the table below.

Model State Farming Stats Having looked at lots of agricultural statistics, the format of the table below gave me the most clarity. If and when we succeed in shopping more local, we might begin to see these numbers move in the positive direction. The next step is for New Englanders to engage with these numbers. These numbers should be constantly checked, crosschecked and updated, as they represent regional food security, health and agricultural jobs. (12-13)

Sales Class	Number of Operations	Acres Operated	Average Farm Size in Acres
$1,000-$9,999	4,800	390,000	81
$10,000-$99,999	2,050	350,000	171
$100,000-$249,000	320	100,000	313
$250,000-$499,000	180	100,000	553
$500,000-$999,999	110	70,000	636
$1,000,000 and up	140	290,000	2,071
Total	7,600	1.3 million	

* * *

11. Agricultural Resources Facts and Statistics, Energy and Environmental Affairs. www.mass.gov/eea/agencies/agr/statistics/
12. Current statistics found at Bureau of Labor Statistics.
www.bls.gov/eag/eag.ma.htm Accessed March 18th 2017.
13. Massachusetts Department of Agricultural Resources,
www.mass.gov/eea/docs/agr/facts/snapshot-of-ma-agriculture.pdf,
New York Times World Almanac

* * *

148. What is one successful approach of a school to support farming? One example is UMass Stockbridge, where community members can buy shares of produce from so-called "community supported agriculture". CSAs are important because farmers are guaranteed revenue from those that buy shares. Second, farmers get paid earlier in the season, which reduces risk and allows them to invest in capital improvements. Third, it helps ensure all produce is sold off, not just the most popular items. Fourth, money spent on food stays local. Massachusetts CSAs experienced a 95% boost from 2007 to 2017. (14)

A. Better Adapt: The Demise of Green Mountain College Before Green Mountain College closed their doors, *College Values Online Metrics* rated their farm in the top five in terms of sustainability and other metrics. Their closure was a step backwards, but the five metrics used that helped Green Mountain College make it to the Top 5 in New England College farms were:

> *significant student involvement*
> *environmentally friendly methods*
> *diversity of production*
> *connection with college instruction*
> *farm sales targeting the college and surrounding community*

B. The Yale University Model It is remarkable that one national award winning college farm is just one acre. It is about the hard work put in, not the size of the farm, which bodes well for colleges with an acre to spare for a farm.

C. Informative Movie *Forgotten Farms: The challenges facing New England's Dairy Farmers, who remain the backbone of the region's agriculture, are examined.* The Friedman School at Tufts University did a very successful screening of this movie.

D: Farm Liability Insurance Course All of a farm or farm family's hard work can go out the window in one lawsuit. A decade or century of a farm family's hard work can all be taken away. However, farm liability insurance courses can help educate farmers on risk managment and help them choose the right insurance company and policy. The web page "Understanding Agricultural Liability" on the website of the Penn State Extension school had a quote that summarizes some of the issue;

> *"As soon as someone enters your property, whether invited or not, you have some form of responsibility for that person's safety."*

The end goal is that New England farmers thrive, despite rising costs, inflation (15) or anything else. (16)

* * *

14. Massachusetts Department of Agricultural Resources,
www.mass.gov/eea/docs/agr/facts/snapshot-of-ma-agriculture.pdf
15. Rising Inflation a Harsh Follow Up to COVID-19 Financing Issue." BU Statehouse Program
16. "Mass. Restaurant Industry is far from a full recovery, even with help." Mutian Qiao
* * *

149. How are the efforts of Greenfield Community College to support local farming a relevant model worthy of study? The *Farm and Food System* program at GCC integrates coursework with "community efforts to support regional food security, local economies, and planning for resiliency." (17) One thing jumped out at me: the fact that they regularly go to other colleges to see what they're doing.

GCC Farmer's Market Intern Students at Greenfield Community college are also eligible to participate as a Community Involved in Sustaining Agriculture (CISA) intern. Tasks include outreach and education to community partner organizations such as Snap and Save, planning and conducting activities, supporting distribution of outreach materials, and more. This might be a good model to learn from.

150. What are some new farm models that schools and colleges might want to teach their students? The table on the facing page is a start. Although the "direct sales" markets grew about 1% from 2007 to 2012, if we're really going to get New England farms humming, while creating the green infrastructure everyone can enjoy, we're going to need to do more. (18)

Farmer's Markets can provide local students with fresh and healthy food and provide employment for them to offset college costs.

* * *

17. Farm and Food Systems Certificate Program, Greenfield Community College. gcc.mass.edu/academics/programs/farm-and-food-systems-certificate
18. New England Small Farm Institute, About NESFI. http://smallfarm.org/main/about_nesfi/

* * *

Table 11
New England Farm Models for Study

Healthy farms are good for everyone. Schools and colleges can help make this happen. Consider that until the Boston Herald did a multi-media piece on Massachusetts farms, (Ottolini, 2019) almost no one knew that 500 were dying. This table is a response to that situation.

Benefits of Thriving Farms	A. Jobs for Ag School Grads and Everyone Else B. Health and Resilience During a Crisis C. Green Space & Healthy Places to Go
Food Delivery Models	1. *Farmers to You* Delivery from Vermont to Ma, with an offering of preset shares. It might be compared to Peapod or Sienna Farms. 2. *Farm Direct Coop* brings produce to Ma. for pickup with various payment methods, including SNAP or volunteering to "pay" for membership. 3. *Mass. Grown Map* A nice online tool with icons identifying various kinds of farm operations. Good for: Shopping. Supporting Ma.
Legislation	The website of the New England Farmer's Union states that *The Land Agriculture Act of 2014* can have great influence on farmers in N.E. Can journalism students do analyses of this act?
Innovative Farm Programs	1. The Greenfield Community College (Ma.) Farm & Food Systems Program integrates class work with the community. (question 149) 2. Beech Hill Farm stand at the College of the Atlantic aims to "close the loop, forming a more sustainable system of food production." 3. The Maine Farm & Sea Coop is a "seafood inclusive" CSA model.
Best College Review Criteria	*Best College Review* picked Hampshire College, Yale and UNH as having three of the twenty best U.S. college farms. Criteria includes: *Integration with the Main Campus* *Sustainability* *Are courses taught at the farm?* *Do students use the farm?* *Integration with the community*
New Farm Business Models	*Boston Public Market* The BPM "shared space" model works for small farms to sell their produce. *Freight Farms* A number of schools operate "freight farms" as a highly space and resource effective way to grow food.

151 to 163
Creating Bright Futures for Vulnerable Groups in New England

"Even in the public schools in those wealthy communities, students get a lot of hand holding when they're applying to college, and a lot of direction on which colleges they're likely to get accepted to. In contrast, many low income students get next to nothing in terms of college counseling and really nothing when it comes to , what are they going to do with their life".

Bill Symonds, Director of Global Pathways, to Robin Young of WBUR, 90.9.

In 1994 as a Senate page, I would sometimes get Senator Berry (D-Peabody. MA.) his sandwiches for lunch, and those are good memories. I never imagined that in 2022 I would be invoking the spirit of his work to act a bridge with the above quote from WBUR to ensure a positive impact for the disabled in the coming pages. But the truth is, his spirit is needed now. If you didn't know him, you can read about him. But, if you knew him, or sat next to him, and he turned and looked at you, sometimes with just one eye, then maybe you understand.

151. How can progressive coursework in agriculture contribute to better mental health for everyone? In so many ways, including the "Top 14"points below. The challenge is to work towards these goals in such a way that the one in seven adults with disabilities can also contribute and benefit.

> *Farm Jobs*
> *Healthy Places for Everyone to Go*
> *Easier Access to Healthy Food*
> *Fight Climate Change with Oxygen Producing Farmland*
> *Stability during External Conflicts*
> *Greater Diversity of Local Produce*
> *Easier Support of Animal Cruelty Standards*
> *Sustainability*
> *Freedom from Fear*
> *Continuing to Be the City on the Hill*

152. How can book ideas be applied to supporting high-quality living for the disabled? There are two main dimensions; special help for the disabled and re-ecognizing how they support the economy as a whole. With competition for resources continuing to intensify everywhere (1), we need to consider using the tools on page 101 to maximize business for both able and disabled New Englanders.

* * *

1. Local Firm to Open Plant in Georgia: Worcester company to spend $43 million on lithium battery operation". (Boston Herald, 1/6/22)

* * *

Testimonial One example of the of the adaptive features at Berry Library at SSU really working is when I was a graduate student there. Because of the adaptive options at the library, they have some tables with an adjustable desktop. What that means is that the table top, or learning surface, can be moved up or down, about 2 feet or so. I'm very tall, so the standard sized table has always been low, and it was nice to be able to move the learning surface to a more comfortable level. If I wanted to work all day, that small modification was a big plus.

153. How exactly do we create Massachusetts farming jobs for the disabled and what is the ultimate goal? We need good examples of successful programs, and then ideally imitate them at locations they can get to. Plain and simple: Becoming the City on the Hill.

A. Correcting Fear and Ignorance of the Law One gritty reality that is tempting to avoid is the law, and mixed feelings and fears that employers may have when it comes to hiring and firing. I'm not a lawyer, but I know Massachusetts and that knowledge of the law or lack thereof is a problem and creates problems. One issue is access. There is no handy guide to the law. That's to say that there is no one volume book to Massachusetts law that I'm aware of. A few years ago I made a decision to get to know the law a little better, and I went online to see what law books were available. All I was able to find was a one hundred volume collection for $5,000. Five grand. I enjoy reading, but there's no way that I'd have time to read one hundred volumes. I spoke to a lawyer, and relayed to her my quandry. She suggested I consider buying the Massachusetts Bar Exam Preparation Book (Quest Bar Review LLC, 2020), which is thick, but readable. I bought it, and chip away at it, but it will take years to acquire even a basic knowledge. There are also the Massachusetts General Laws online, and they are a helpful tool, but are really only for reference.

B. Dawn of the One Volume Law Book? Or Just a Course? I write the above paragraph because I do have an inherent trust in the faith and goodwill of Massachusetts residents towards the disabled. I really do. And, I believe that if people know the law, they will follow it, because most people don't like trouble. However, if we are going to serve the disabled, employers, disabled employers, job trainers and disabled job trainers to the best of our ability, we can't avoid the subject.

154. How do we make supporting the disabled synonymous with supporting the economy? Everyone wins when we go "full adult" and sink our teeth into how to make the economy work for everyone. The table on the next page consolidates some information on that in one page. Understanding the employment categories and subcategories is a start. A healthy economy supports the disabled and the disabled support a healthy economy. A year of studying this stuff and I've only scratched the surface. Consider how many New England farms were dying (Boston Herald. Ottolini. 2019) and that almost no one knew. Some stats say that as many as 1 in 7 American adults are disabled. At the same time, many employers are having a hard time finding workers, which is why this book advocates the role of community colleges in assuring we adapt to the needs of the disabled and the economy.

One Lesson Learned

The U.S. Small Business Administration defines small businesses as those with 1-499 employees, and big business as 500 employees and up. After spending about 500 hours with the statistics on the website of the U.S. Small Business Administration, one thing jumped out at me; a great number of the small businesses have only one or two employees. What that means is that many small businesses are often looking for a few quality employees, or sometimes just one.

In the past we had found a role in society and accommodated for those with disabilities to feel productive once more. Something we must do once again.

Table 12:
Support the Disabled, Support the Economy

The economy supports the disabled and the disabled support the economy. You can go to the U. S. Small Business Administration website and click on your state's economic profile. "Total Private Employment" stats on that site are 2020 and previous -- not in 2021 NE state reports. This chart is designed to support the disabled in a way that is up to the standards of the late State Senator Fred Berry. So everyone wins.

Acknowledging the Change	Competition for resources will continue to intensify everywhere.
The Green Network Principle	Thriving Mass. farms are good for everyone, but especially for the disabled or those having a hard time. Or in unstable times. A farm off almost every exit, a go to farm close to home. The website *Mass Grown* enables location and support of farms near you.
Top 5 Massachusetts Employment Categories	Below are five of the eighteen employment categories on the USSBA website "Total Private Employment"table. Consider that when the Boston Herald's did a piece on how 500 Massachusetts farms were dying ("Massachusetts Farms Struggle to Stay Afloat", Ottolini), almost no one knew. This is reason enough to pay attention to the economy and work together. 1. Health Care and Social Assistance 2. Accomodation and Food Services 3. Professional, Scientific and Technical Services 4. Retail Trade 5. Manufacturing Self-Employed: 6-12% (Cape and Islands 12-29%)
U.S. Small Business Administration Sources	U.S. Small Business Administration source websites can be used to understand the needs of workers, disabled workers, employers, disabled employers and the economy. *ACS: American Community Survey* *ASE: Annual Survey of Entrepreneurs* *BEA: Bureau of Economic Analysis* *BDM: Business Employment Dynamics* *BLS: Bureau of Labor Statistics* *CPS: Current Population Survey* *Call Reports, Federal Deposit Insurance Corporation* *FFIEC: Federal Financial Institutions Examination Council* *ITA: International Trade Administration.* *Nonemployer Statistics* *Statistics of US Businesses.*

Table 13:

Understanding Unemployment Rating Systems

When we talk about the unemployment rate, it's important we understand exactly what official numbers mean. For example, in Maine, community college enrollment has gone from 10,000 to 18,000, with many being trained for specific jobs (2). However, the value and specific importance of job creation is more clear when we understand how many people need work, and what their status was before their new job.

U-3	This is what BLS (Bureau of Labor and Statistics) calls the "official unemployment rate." It represents unemployed workers who are actively searching for a new job.
U-4	This is the total unemployed plus "discouraged workers." Discouraged workers are those who have given up looking for a job because they think there are not any available for them.
U-5	This is the total unemployed, plus discouraged workers, plus "other persons marginally attached to the labor force." The marginally attached are people who are neither working nor looking for work, but indicate they want and are available for a job and have looked for work sometime in the last year. But they aren't counted as unemployed, because they didn't actively search for work in the last four weeks.
U-6	U-6 includes all of the above groups — total unemployed, discouraged workers and the marginally attached — *plus* part-time workers who say they would like to be working more, but for economic reasons could only find part-time work.

(3)

* * *

2. "Eastern Maine Community College Enrollment at Historic High for Fourth Straight Year", Bangor Daily News, October 5th 2012.
3. Bureau of Labor Statistics

* * *

Comme Sisyphe by Honoré Daumier

155. Why is the work of the Salem State economics department so valuable and crucial? Graduating generations of young people with no knowledge of mortgage and finance is simply not an option anymore. Young people desperately need to acquire knowledge about personal finance, including mortgage, finance, renting and credit if they are to survive and thrive in the world.

The first thing to know about the Salem State University Center for Economic Development is the SM.AR.T. program, which is a seminar for teaching personal finance to college students. Offered once or twice a year, the seminars attract fifteen to thirty students who then learn all about ways to best manage their money. The Salem State Center for Economic Education also offers free workshops to K-12 teachers on how to teach personal finance to students and provide teachers with more tools and updated information they can bring back to their classrooms.

156. How does Salem State choose the books for the courses and why is their source important for other educators to know about? The SSU economics department uses resources from the *Council for Economic Education* (4) and many other sources. That's good news for schools or colleges that are looking to introduce personal programs; the CEE can help with choosing all the books and materials, which means that dimension of program implementation doesn't have to be so hard.

157. What regular coursework does the department offer for teaching personal finance? According to one professor in the department, "The department offers Economics of Personal Financial Decisions as one of the economics elective courses students can take during their regular semester and is working on developing personal finance course open to all Non-economics majors to take, in combination with workshops and other initiatives on campus to provide students with more information they need regarding financial literacy".

Places with largest increases in homeless people

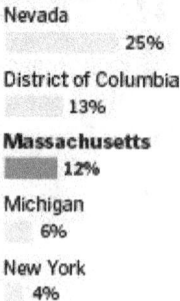
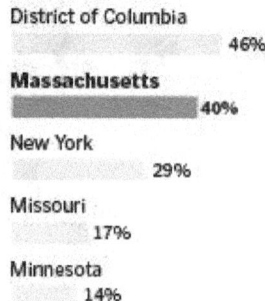

2013-2014

Nevada
25%

District of Columbia
13%

Massachusetts
12%

Michigan
6%

New York
4%

2007-2014

District of Columbia
46%

Massachusetts
40%

New York
29%

Missouri
17%

Minnesota
14%

SOURCE: Department of Housing and Urban Development   OLIVIA HALL FOR THE BOSTON GLOBE

* * *

4.The informatiion in the three questions above came about through reading about the program and doing a face 'to face intereview with one member of the Salem State economics department. The professor then followed up by sending me a very informative email about their programs.

* * *

Hunger on Campus Of the twenty-nine state colleges and universities, twenty-four operate food pantries or have partnerships with food banks. Forty-five percent of the colleges reported a rise in student homelessness over the last year. Most Massachusetts colleges state they have students living in shelters, cars, or "couch surfing." In some extremes, students are living in 24hr businesses such as Dunkin' Donuts and McDonald's, or in the woods during warmer weather. (5) According to federal data 1,020 students at Massachusetts' public colleges and universities are homeless or at risk of homelessness. (6)

One college has a campus fund that provides low-income students with $7 vouchers for the college cafeteria, while the University of Massachusetts Amherst created supply closets with toiletries and other household items for needy students. (7)

Public College Commuters The information above is from 2013-2016, when this book was originally published. What has happened to the statistics since then, what policies have changed as the result of Covid-19, is unknown. What I do know is public college commuter students are a very overlooked demographic, and being cut off from classes and food is a big deal. Not to mention the Commuter Lounge.

Council for Economic Education Both SSU and BSU have models that can be useful in battling student debt and homelessness, in two ways. First of all, the seminars teach students how to manage money. Second, the department also partners to put together seminars on planning for college and minimizing student debt. In the words of a Salem State professor;

"The Center for Economic Education together with Massachusetts Council on Economic Education conducted a three-hour workshop on College & Career Readiness for secondary educators that addresses the necessary skills and knowledge students need to establish a pathway to success, informed by economic decision making and utilizing the Council for Economic Education's Virtual Economics Version 4.5 collection on lesson plans and activities."

158. What can schools do to fight animal cruelty? Promting existing efforts on college radio certainly has helped and helps. The reduction of cat, dog and other kills in shelters nationwide from 3.6 to 2.1 million is a great success, and One could look at different arenas of this fight, such as the firsthand accounts of when members of the Northeast Animal Shelter in Salem Ma. drove to Georgia to rescue, care for and place eighty dogs. See "Underground Railroad Smuggles Dogs from Shelters to the Northeast" in the *New York Post* for that story. (8) I was proud to share the tales of some of these efforts on 91.7 FM, WMWM.

* * *

5. Louise Kennedy, "Mass. Public Campuses See More Hungry And Homeless Students", WBUR, January 24, 2017. www.wbur.org

6. Matt Rocheleau, "Their Budgets Strained, Students Turn to Campus Food Pantries", The Boston Globe, December 15, 2014

7. Danielle Douglas Gabriel, "Why Massachusetts is creating its own student debt counseling unit", The Washington Post, November 24, 2015

8. Arin Greenwood, "ASPCA reveals historic data for shelter pets: Adoptions are up, euthanasia is down". March 9, 2017, www.today.com/

* * *

Table 14
The Frustrated Mom's 12 Pack

K-12 Education	1. Full recess, fun physical education and walk-to school programs (Safe Routes) means kids feel good during the day. Plus, those programs are great for inclusion and Mom doesn't have to worry about her kid getting picked on. 2. The kids love Spanish class because they get to read out loud in the language, and they actually learn to speak.
Community Colleges	3. Apprenticeships at the community colleges mean there's a chance the kids can find a mentor in the trades while learning in classroom time. (See question 132) 4. Thanks to youtube videos on the community college channels that follow the model of the AMPitUp! Program, (question 164) Mom can learn about industry partnerships.
Agriculture and Manufacturing Jobs	5. Responses by schools to support New England agriculture (Table 11) means more farm jobs, so the kids or Mom might get a summer or a full-time job. Yes! Yes! Yes! 6. Growth in manufacturing (see Table 15) spurred by college programs means family members can find manufacturing jobs, which means more family income.
Conservation	7. Conservation groups and students work together to set aside big state and national parks. The schools study USAfacts.org, USAspending.gov and other transparency websites, so Moms can make sure priorities get funded. 8. College environmental departments, clubs and idealistic politicians get support to help everyone enjoy our natural wonders, with affordable lodging at the parks and low fees.
College Radio	9. College radio plays fresh new music, has lots of specialty shows: talk, college sports and local djs piping in the tunes and the latest updates about stuff close to home. 10. After four years of college radio, Mom's son expresses himself well and is a great listener. Plus, he has helped to support lots of causes that really needed support.
Supporting the Disabled	11. The disabled get behind steps forward in manufacturing (Table 15), farming (Table 11) and conservation (Table 6), so Moms with disabled kids have more job prospects. 12. Schools embed guidance counseling into the school day, so the disabled and all students can find a career.

159. What are some existing successes in education that support quality of life for the elderly? It seems appropriate to begin by saying that I have seen the elderly in a full range of different kinds of struggles and living situations. and so, below are some existing, successful educational models that have worked for others, in the hope someone else might make use of them.

The Economics of Happiness & Grandmother's Colleges

In the movie the *Economics of Happiness,* an older Indian woman talked about the value of "grandmother's colleges", schools where older women could share their stories and ensure that local knowledge, "which is knowledge of life", would never die. (9) The closest New England existing model to grandmothers colleges might be the Explorers Club of Salem State University, where students over 50 are taught by SSU professors.

Timebanks and Seniors

Time banking is a way for older people that may not be able to hold a job do what they love, receive services and be part of a supportive group. See question 131 on page 78 for more.

University of Texas Social Security Course Model

Grandparents can take the course to figure out which of the 82 different paths to enrollment in the program makes sense for them. (10)

The Two Lessons of WBUR

The quality of some of the programming on WBUR, 90.9 FM is of such a high quality that it makes people who quote some of their guests sound smart. After listening to an interview on WBUR about the importance of guidance in the schools is key, and how it can insure all the members of the flock are getting good support, it seems appropriate to leave the takeaway quote below.

"The average American school now has one guidance counselor for every 500 students. In some places the ratio is far more dire — nearly 1,000 kids for every counselor....I think it's a massive crisis...I think it's really the black hole in the American education system."

Bill Symonds, director of Global Pathways Institute, to WBUR's Robin Young.

Intergenerational Communication

A second informative interview on WBUR featured the only member of the Massachusetts House of Representatives with a family member in prison. She has been touched by extreme violence multiple times, and she and a stressed out young person emphasized the role of intergenerational communication in helping to prevent it from happening to others. The interview is an example of what college radio can be.

* * *

9. The idea of grandmother's colleges was featured in the 2011 movie The Economics of Happiness. Directors: Helena Norberg-Hodge, Steven Gorelick, and John Page. Production: Local Futures. Music: Florian Frick. Editors: Anna Fricke, Army Armstrong and Meredith Holch. www.imdb.com

10. Texas, University of, Extended Campus Course: "Maximizing Social Security", https://informalu-texas.edu/classes/maximizing-social-security

* * *

160. How might the BNI model of sharing knowledge work in the classroom? BNI, or Business Networking International is a group I belonged to promote my business, and it's clear that their model of knowledge sharing could work well for young people. At every morning breakfast, two members would give a ten minute presentation about their career and profession. Our group of fifty or so members was represented by one member of each profession, and every day two members gave ten minute minute presentations about their careers and profession. It was informative to hear carpenters, credit card processors, mechanics and members of other professions tell their story.

I thought of this group of BNI to consider is guidance counseling in the schools is in short supply. I became aware of the lack of guidance counselors from Bill Symonds, director of the Global Pathways Institute said on *Here & Now* with Robin Young;

"I'm talking about re-configuring how we deliver education; we want to make it a lot more relevant". As for the why of why we need change, he said; "I think it's a massive crisis....I think it's really the black hole in the American education system."

See: www.wbur.org/hereandnow/2015/01/16/guidance-counselor-crisis

161. What are the top ways parents, students and educators can learn about New England manufacturing? First of all, we need to be aware of the quote of the President of the University of Massachusetts of Lowell, when she said;

"The manufacturing industry in Massachusetts is facing a critical shortfall in skilled workers...over the next decade, nearly 3.5 million manufacturing jobs (nationwide) will likely need to be filled, and the skills gap is expected to result in 2 million of those jobs going unfilled."

Learn About The Credit Transfer Systems Parents and students might consider getting familiar with the credit transfer systems in each of the six New England states. In Massachusetts this is called MassTransfer and in New Hampshire is NH Transfer. The other four NE states have their own system.

Transferring Credit by Major Although the credit transfer systems are relatively streamlined, transfer of credit for a major can be challenging., as in some cases the department decides whether or not to accept the credits.

Understand the Articulation Agreements The various articulation agreements have changed vocational education. They mean that if students can prove proficiency in a vocational subject, they receive a certificate, and can receive credit for it at a community college. (11) See page 86 for the list of skills that are recognized in Massachusetts.

Flagship University Programs UNH, the University of Maine and the University of Connecticut train the skilled workers of the future and support manufacturers. The programs at each of the three colleges are different; see the table on page 110 for the centers whose work you might choose to learn more about.

* * *

11. Massachusetts State Articulation Agreement Between Massachusetts Community Colleges and Massachusetts Chapter 74 Approved Secondary Career/Vocational Technical Programs, Massachusetts Community Colleges. www.masscc.org/sites/default/files/Engineering.pdf

* * *

All these changes mean that going to a vocational school has a whole world of new options. However, learning about the articulation agreements is a daunting process, because some are between schools and some are between school systems. Nevertheless, all of the developments respond to the concern of Globe writer Jay Fitzgerald in his article, which expressed concern about the skills of workers matching employers. (12)

Read About Industry Partnerships There are a growing number of industry partnerships, and one example of which is an industry partnership between Pratt-Whitney and York Country Community College, whereby YCCC trains workers for specific jobs in the Pratt-Whitney plant. The industry gets the skilled workers, the college gets support from the industry partner, and families see their children gain employment.

Learn About Apprenticeships The growth of apprenticeships at community colleges throughout New England was brand new to me when I learned about them in 2016, and I'm sure that many parents and students are unaware as well. I had the opportunity to speak to an administrator at Vermont Tech, and I was told that whereas employers might not have had the time to train employees in the past, the training VTC now offers makes it worth it for them, because the 144 hours of classroom time supplements what the mentor's apprentice teaches. So, the mentor, be he or she a plumber or HVAC person, is not stuck having to explain every little thing to the apprentice.

Manufacturing Extension Partnership (MEP) Trainings Each of the six MEPs in New England, including but not restricted to the 7-8 week manufacturing training programs on the campus of UMass Lowell and others.

162. How is the MassDevelopment AMP it up! Program so important to advanced manufacturing? Since the program launch in 2013, MassDevelopment has offered grants to 20 partnerships composed of employment and workforce investment boards, manufacturers, community colleges, and youth organizations, to offer activities and events aimed at encouraging young people to pursue careers in manufacturing.

The recognition of the Commonwealth that there was a need to educate young people on the opportunities in manufacturing was a good first step, as manufacturers have been crying out for years that they can't find the skilled workers. The article by Jay Fitzgerals was a start, but to hear it directly from community college presidents was something else.

"Through the AMP it up! grants, we will tap into various resources within community-based programs to further educate and inform students, teachers, and organizations about the range of opportunities advanced manufacturing will provide for this generation and future generations as we work towards sustainable and long-term economic growth."

The value of the AMPitUp! model in promoting manufacturing is explained well on the website of Mass Development. (13)

* * *

12. Jay Fitzgerald, Worker's Skills Aren't Matching Available Jobs", *The Boston Globe*, December 17, 2003. www.northeastern.edu
13. "Five Massachusetts Schools Win AMP it up! Challenge". May 18, 2018. www.massdevelopment.org

* * *

Table 15

On Campus Support and Promotion of Manufacturing

"The manufacturing industry in Massachusetts is facing a critical shortfall in skilled workers...over the next decade, nearly 3.5 million manufacturing jobs (nationwide) will likely need to be filled, and the skills gap is expected to result in 2 million of those jobs going unfilled."

NE Manufacturing Training Centers	UMaine: The Advanced Manufacturing Center UNH: The John Olson Center UConn offers a minor in manufacturing
Maximizing and Securing Social Security	*SS Course* With 82 different pathways to enrollment in Social Security, the University of Texas course is a model for helping workers choose the right pathway. Below, the SS Tracker allows us to protect benefits of manufacturing workers, and everyone. ssa.gov/policy/social-security-long-term-financial-outlook.html
MassDevelopment and AMPitUP!	"The AMP it up! initiative includes an annual competition that challenges middle and high school students to create a three-minute video about a local manufacturer. "AMP it up! matching grants.....educate young people and adults about career options in advanced manufacturing."
Manufacturing Extension Partnership Trainings	Manufacturing Extension Partnership (MEP) teach basic CNC (computer numerical control) in just seven weeks. Each NE state has an equivalent. **Note:** According to a MEP rep I interviewed in 2017, UMass Lowell and Worcester Polytechnical are the only Massachusetts schools outfitted for such trainings.
Successes and Opportunities	1. Boston College added a School of Engineering in 2019. 2. Massachusetts Bay Community College offers S.T.E.M. pro-gramming, which supports the skilled manufacturing workforce. 3. Some recommend embedding counseling into the school day (page 98), which could enable learning about opportunities in manufacturing. 4. The People's Academy in Boston is a private model for teaching vocational skills. 5. One million veterans are coming home & steps to accommo-date them (pgs 121-131) can create new candidates.

163. What is the role of The Boston Herald in supporting education and journalism in New England? When The Boston Herald declared bankruptcy in December of 2017, it set off alarm bells and essentially created this question. In 2023, it seems a review of examples of their contributions to this book is in order. The quote below in the Boston Herald on 1/8/18, page 14 brought up just how precarious physical and financial security is for too many.

"For those of us who are financially insecure, who worry about their health, and who never found true friends, the need for security, safety and community are real."

- Gina Barrega

Boston Herald Top 5 Book Contributions

Started as one two sided sheet for stagecoach listings in 1825, the 40-48 page magazine or "tabloid" format is train or coffee shop friendly. While travelling to 70 college sports events games and three practices around New England, the Herald was a welcome companion. Countless other writers have contributed to this book, but the role of the Herald has been unique.

1. *Project Ground Floor* The reprint of a *Chicago Tribune* article on an Illinois shared home ownership model called *Project Ground Floor was* groundbreaking. model can work for adjuncts and the disabled in particular, but also for young people looking to pay a small mortgage rather than high rent.

2. *A Model of Fairness* When the woes of one state agency were all being blamed on one employee, the *Boston Herald* was not having it. They called the union representative and and let him defend the employee in his care. Going forward, we are going to need this kind of discernment.

3. *Massachusetts Farm Support* The multimedia piece by Megan Ottolini about 500 dying Massachusetts farms, and many others struggling, inspired the creation of a special section in support of Massachusetts agriculture on pages 94-97.

4. *Saving Social Security* Thanks to an article in the Herald about the threat of the Social Security trust fund running dry by 2030, book responses were integrated into this book. An entire new chapter on Social Security was also revamped in response to that article in another book, *Ideas for America - Let the Sun In.*

5. *Fighting Animal Cruelty* A July 2020 piece on federally funded animal experiments asked hard questions, shared uncomfortable truths and details, and then *followed up* with a second piece. As for the animals in the cages, the work of the Herald was their only hope. Is that not true journalism?

On the wall of editor Rachel Cohen's former office at *The Boston Herald* was a pic of the front page of the Herald from December 4, 1982, which reads "YOU BET WE'RE ALIVE!". The only problem is that 1982 is a long time ago, and the value and style of journalism the Herald need to be remembered.

Senior citizens enrolled in classes learning new tricks, but what can they be teaching the younger generation? The Explorers Club at Salem State University

is one New England college that caters to older students.

Dartmouth University has been a top notch institution for those who can afford it, but we need to be aware of the state colleges that provide a fair shake for those who are trying to strengthen our middle class.

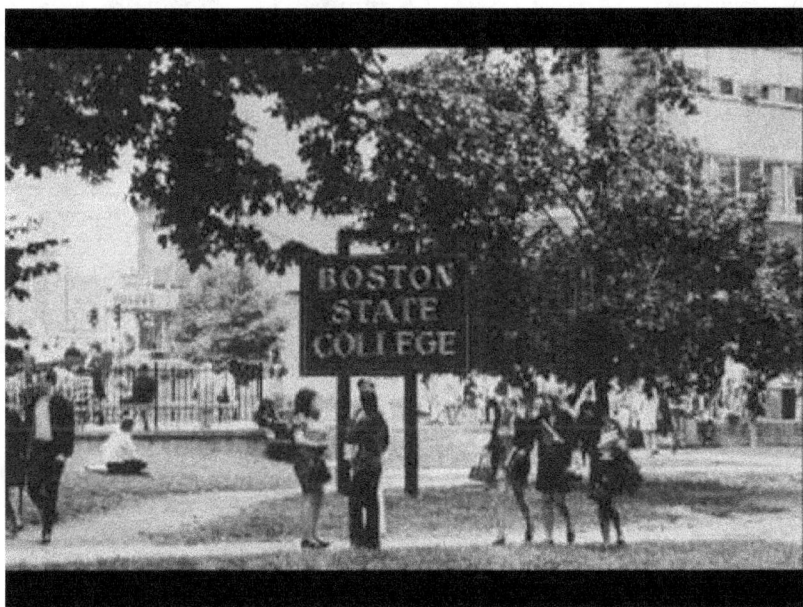

One of the many state colleges that have closed over the years that removed an option for restoring the middle class.

164 to 175
The Present and Future of STEM in New England Education

164. What is the true impact of S.T.E.M. on job creation? Standing for Science, Technology, Engineering and Math, S.T.E.M. jobs represent a significant portion of the jobs of the future. This section gives voice to the experts and highlights a few dimension to consider.

The discussion around STEM jobs is intense, because according to some, the jobs to be had in this category represent the future of employment for a vast number of people. There are a lot of things to consider before anyone can decide whether diving head first into a STEM career, including:

1. *Know what STEM Is* Students need to understand the selling points of STEM, but also the best jobs out there in its fields.

2 *Listen to the Experts* Know what is being said about its outlook, generally and by specific entities, including the Economics and Statistics Administration and the U.S. Department of Commerce, but also faculty at schools and colleges.

3. *Compare STEM Career Tracks* Compare STEM careers with the outlooks for other high-paying careers for college graduates.

165. What is STEM? *The most widely-cited definition is: "STEM education is an interdisciplinary approach to learning where rigorous academic concepts are coupled with real-world lessons as students apply science, technology, engineering, and mathematics in contexts that make connections between school, community, work, and the global enterprise."(1)*

166. What is the main STEM Selling Point, and what are the projected job increases? According to a paper written by faculty at Carnegie Mellon;

"In 2010, there were 7.6 million STEM workers in the United States, representing about 1 in 18 workers." (2)

This is a great numerical starting point when discussing percentage increases. In the event that STEM workers come to represent 1 in 16 or one in 14 workers, we'll be able to see the shift.

* * *

1. Tsupros, N., Kohler, R., & Hallinen, J. (2009). STEM education: A project to identify the missing components. Pittsburgh, PA: Intermediate Unit 1: Center for STEM Education and Leonard Gelfand Center for Service Learning and Outreach, Carnegie Mellon University.

2. Langdon, D., McKittrick, G., Beede, D., Khan, B., & Doms, M. (2011). STEM: Good Jobs Now and for the Future. Washington, DC: Office of the Chief Economist, Economics and Statistics Administration, U.S. Department of Commerce. Retrieved from www.esa.doc.gov/sites/default/files/stemfinalyjuly14_1.pdf

* * *

STEM vs. Other Occupations: Compared to all of the other occupations, STEM careers – individually and collectively – have a higher percentage of increase. What this overshadows is the aggregate factor, because it's a few jobs versus all the rest from all other fields. Some of the other fields' jobs are likely to have similar projections as STEM – if not better. I need to say that parents and students are better off understanding not just the increase in jobs in STEM, but rather the trends within the individual fields of STEM.

Different Types of STEM: It is also important for young people to consider that while there is a 62% projected increase in Biomedical Engineer jobs, there is only a 16% increase projected for Mathematics. These considerations are pertinent when choosing which field of STEM to pursue.

167. What are some salary considerations with regard to STEM jobs? Those with only a high school diploma are expected to make 59.6% more per hour in a STEM job than a non-STEM job. This is not surprising. Yet it is impressive that those with a graduate degree are expected to make more than 12.3%! It is a positive outlook for young people who enter STEM jobs and careers, as they are likely to make more per hour regardless of the level of education they have attained.

168. What are the best jobs in STEM? According to a *U.S. News and World Report* article, the 25 Best STEM Jobs range from software developer with an average salary of $100,000 to Architect at number 25 with a average salary of $76,000. Out of the 25 jobs the article lists,

1. Software developer
9. Civil Engineer
24. Anthropologist
25. Architect

For students and parents that are looking to learn more about careers in STEM, the complete *U.S. News and World Report* article is a good place to start (3).

169. What do people say about STEM? People say a lot of things. Much of the public enthusiasm for STEM education rests on the assumption that these fields are rich in job opportunity, although it's important to bear in mind that STEM is an expansive category, spanning many disciplines and occupations, from software engineers and data scientists to geologists, astronomers and physicists. What that means is that we need to dig a little deeper, which is the reason for this section of the book.

* * *

3. U.S. News & World Report. (2018, April 18). Best STEM Jobs. Retrieved from U.S. News & World Report - Money: https://money.usnews.com/careers/best-jobs/rankings/best-stem-jobs
* * *

170. With regards to the future of STEM, what are the conclusions of the Economics and Statistics Administration? According to an ECA report, the future for STEM is bright.

"Science, technology, engineering and mathematics (STEM) workers drive our nation's innovation and competitiveness by generating new ideas, new companies and new industries [...] over the past 10 years, growth in STEM jobs was three times as fast as growth in non-STEM jobs. STEM workers are also less likely to experience joblessness [...]". (4)

171. What is one critical conclusion from a Steve Lohr article? Bottom Line: The number of graduates with a STEM background tends to outpace job openings, with Computer science as the exception. Below shows the Categories of STEM Jobs:, showing total graduates and available jobs.

Category	Graduates	Available Jobs	Mismatch
Life Sciences	183K	12K	171K more graduates than jobs
Engineering	169K	51K	118K more graduates than jobs
Physical Sciences	43K	9K	34K more graduates than jobs
Mathematical Sciences	33K	7K	26K more graduates than jobs
Computer Science	107K	108K	1k more jobs than graduates

(5)

Impact Lohr!

How disturbing! Research data directly contradicts the projected job increases mentioned before. This supports Steve Lohr's conclusion and provides another perspective for young people to consider. Computer Science is where the growth is expected; specifically, Computer Science for Biomedical Engineering may be the way to go. That said, this is also where good guidance counseling comes in.

In the meantime, a few New England colleges seem to have heard Mr. Lohr; Boston College went ahead and added a College of Enginering in 2019 and Massachusetts Bay Community College now offers STEM programming.

* * *

4. U.S. News & World Report. (2018, April 18). Best STEM Jobs. Retrieved from U.S. News & World Report - Money: https://money.usnews.com/careers/best-jobs/rankings/best-stem-jobs

5. Lohr, Steve (2017, November 1). Where the STEM Jobs Are (and Where They Aren't). The New York Times. Retrieved from https://mobile.nytimes.com/2017/11/01/education/edlife/stem-jobs-industry-careers.html
* * *

172. What were some words of caution from Fareed Zakaria? Fareed Zakaria, a columnist for *The Washington Post* and author of "In Defense of a Liberal Education", wrote an article called "Why America's Obsession with STEM Education is Dangerous". For me, the takeaway quote from that article was the following.

"A broad general education helps foster critical thinking and creativity. Exposure to a variety of fields produces synergy and cross fertilization. Yes, science and technology are crucial components of this education, but so are English and philosophy." (6)

I was glad to come across the above sentiment with regards to the human condition, but I have a slightly different perspective. I too worry about Americans becoming mindless, dehumanized robots, but I don't express that concern through opposing STEM education. Rather, through supporting it. Nonetheless, I'm glad Fareed said his piece: that the world needs more than technology and science!

173. What are some takeaways from "Seven Facts About the STEM Workforce, put out by the PEW Research Organization? According to an article on their website, employment in science, technology, engineering and math (STEM) occupations has grown 79% since 1990, from 9.7 million to 17.3 million, outpacing overall U.S. job growth.

There's no single standard for which jobs count as STEM, and this may contribute to a number of misconceptions about who works in STEM and the difference that having a STEM-related degree can make in workers' pocketbooks. (6) It is now abundantly clear that any serious discussion of STEM's influence on job creation needs to include an understanding of the facts presented below: (7)

1. STEM workers enjoy a pay advantage.

2. Roughly a third of STEM workers have not completed a bachelor's or higher.

3. Half of workers with STEM training have a non-STEM job.

4. STEM training in college gets you higher pay in STEM and non-STEM jobs.

174. According to College Choice, which of the 50 highest paying careers for college graduates are STEM jobs? In the article titled "The 50 Highest Paying Careers for College Graduates", many are STEM jobs, but there are many other careers that offer salaries high enough to support life after college.

* * *

6. Fareed Zakaria, "Why America's obsession with STEM Education is Dangerous". The Washington Post, March 26, 2015. That and many other articles by Fareed can also be found at his own website.

7. Graf, N., Fry, R., & Funk, C. (2018, January 9), "7 facts about the STEM workforce", Pew Research Center,. www.pewresearch.org/fact-tank/2018/01/09/7-facts-about-the-stem-workforce/
* * *

Non-STEM examples to highlight from this list are, from highest paying to lowest paying, including outliers (first is STEM, sorry) and average salary ranges (8), are below. See Salary.com for all eighteen STEM jobs, with salary numbers. Below are twelve of those eighteen jobs from the Salary.com "Top 50"list.

      1. Petroleum Engineering
      15. Economist
      24. Construction Management
      26. Operations and Supply Chain Management
      31. Industrial Designer (9)

As they state on their website, *College Choice* also offers numerous free online resources to help you in your college search, including;

> *student-centered college ranking*
> *admissions advice, scholarship*
> *financial aid information*
> *and much, much, more.*

175. What are existing efforts to promote STEM programming at New England schools and colleges? Clearly, when discussing education policy, we need to keep the potential for job growth in agriculture, manufacturing, apprenticeships, industry partnerships in mind – along with the impact of STEM. STEM should not discount the need for continued open discussions about other ways to grow jobs. If we use our minds and work together, schools and colleges can create more clear pathways to employment for both young students and adults.

It is important for schools and colleges to be a major part of the job creation solution, and we need to look to our New England schools to find what role they will play in STEM job creation, both in terms of creating opportunities and in effectively informing parents and students of the options students now have.

* * *

8. Graf, N., Fry, R., & Funk, C. "7 facts about the STEM workforce", Pew Research Center,. www.pewresearch.org/fact-tank/2018/01/09/7-facts-about-the-stem-workforce/ January 9, 2018

9. "50 Highest Paying Careers for College Graduates", College Choice, www.collegechoice.net/50-highest-paying-careers-college-graduates/

* * *

176 to 206
Veterans and New England Education

"80% of manufacturers report having a hard time finding quality workers. At the same time, we have a million veterans coming home over the next four years."

Jennifer McNelly, President, The Manufacturing Institute

With over 1,000,000 veterans are coming home, including 40,000 to New England. connecting veterans to employment is a challenge and opportunity. (1) With schools in heavy competition for new students, returning veterans are a source of potential new customers. They are also a potential source of skilled labor. With regards to education and serving veterans, this book focuses on:

> 1) what existing programs can do for veterans
> 2) what veterans can do for the skilled labor shortage

176. What can New England colleges do to best serve veterans? Somehow, New England veterans need to become aware of apprenticeships, manufacturing work, other needs for skilled workers, and how New England colleges are responding. Community colleges are a key component for connecting veterans to training and jobs, which is one reason this book supports those colleges.

"I can't tell you how many guys that I know in the last five years that have really struggled coming out of the military and being told they just don't have the experience that they need".
> - Youtube video: A Future for Veterans in Manufacturing

177. What are the specific roles of community colleges in boosting the fortunes of New England veterans? Community colleges are the closest thing to "people's colleges", institutions whose role has changed in recent years. One role of this book is to advocate for community colleges and one of the groups they serve; existing and returning veterans. Some advantages of community colleges include:

> *ease of enrollment*
> *effective credit transfer systems*
> *apprenticeships*
> *industry partnerships*
> *support of veterans centers*

* * *

1. "The changing face of America's veteran population", Pew Research. www.pewresearch.org/fact-tank/2017/11/10/the-changing-face-of-americas-veteran-population/

* * *

178. How is boosting the fortunes of veterans similar to boosting the fortunes of adjuncts or the disabled? Just as working together to maximize the lives of adjuncts (see table on page 32) or the disabled (pages 98-101) is good for everyone, so too are steps forward for veterans. That's to say that supporting veterans doesn't have to be a drain on resources, but rather integrating them can be a boost for our need for skilled workers. In fact, even the practice of looking at the tables for supporting veterans and adjuncts and imagining the possibilities can be good practice for seeing the possiblities for both healthy veterans and those with extreme needs.

179. How do I distinguish between healthy veterans and those with extreme needs? When I began to imagine ways to support veterans, I thought there might be a few million, but there are about 20 million veterans nationwide, which means there are quite a few in New England. According to an article in Pew Research, the majority of these are Gulf War era. As a friend once remarked; she "didn't know any veterans who didn't have some level of PTSD", and I have the same observation of most of those who have been in combat. For those who are basically healthy, using existing support systems with the creative application of the "The Frustrated Mom's 12 Pack" on page 106 is a good start.

The Man from Maine When I read about the existing support systems for veterans on campus, I think of a video filmed outside a VA hospital in Maine, in which an utterly distressed man shares his pain. (2) We should correctly estimate the value some veteran's counselors currently have supporting veterans like this, but many non-veteran Americans also have poor health, which is why I share info on both.

180. What can we learn from veterans on college campuses in the past and how much of that applies to the present? I think there always have been and always will be very different perspectives on life between those who have suffered terribly and those who have not. However, the ideal outcome is not for these two groups to ostracize each other, but ideally to learn from and support each other.

* * *

2. Jeff Paradis' Powerful Plea To Maine Veterans-You're F'in Worth It!, Youtube video: www.youtube.com/watch?v=jDpDZW4F9bg

* * *

Suffering of Americans

1. 65% of Americans take prescriptions daily; 43% are mood altering. (3)

2. Forty million Americans in the U.S. will experience an impairment because of an anxiety condition this year. Only four million of those diagnosed with a stress or anxiety condition will receive treatment." (4)

3. The number of Americans reporting extreme stress continues to be high; 20 percent said their stress is in an 8, 9 or 10 scale.

4. The opioid epidemic claimed over 2,000 lives in my home state of Massachusetts in 2017 alone, which is more than the number of Massachusetts residents that died during the entire Vietnam conflict.

5. Nearly 45,000 lives were lost to suicide in 2016 (5) and suicide rates went up more than 30% in half of states since 1999 (6), including Vermont and New Hampshire. (7)

6. The Social Security Trust Fund is at risk of running out of money, which could devastate many of the 70 million Americans currently in the program, as well as the next 70 million. That would impact almost half of American households.
  See: ssa.gov/policy/social-security-long-term-financial-outlook.html

* * *

3. Anxiety Centre
4. A Call to Revolutionize Chronic Pain Care in America. May Day Report
5. "Suicide Rising Across the U.S.", Centers for Disease Control and Protection. www.cdc.gov/vital-signs/suicide/index.html
6. Ibid.
7. Suicide Rising Across the U.S.", Centers for Disease Control and Protection. www.cdc.gov/vital-signs/suicide/index.html

* * *

Suffering of American Veterans

1. 82% of Operation Enduring Freedom - OEF or Operation for Iraqi Freedom - OIF veterans report chronic pain

2. 1,573 veterans have suffered major loss of limb amputations from battle injuries since 2010.

3. The National Coalition for Homeless Veterans believes housing and employment opportunities are a top priority for homeless veterans.

4. Veterans' past exposure to chemicals (Agent Orange, contaminated water), radiation (nuclear weapons, X-rays), air pollutants (burn pit smoke, dust), occupational hazards (asbestos, lead), warfare agents (chemical and biological weapons), noise, and vibration increase their risk of health problems even years after the assault. (8)

5. According to the *National Coalition for Homeless Veterans*, Veterans' successful reintegration into civilian life stem from community involvement, access to resources, and support from peers.

* * *

8. Maria Olenick, Monica Flowers, Valerie J. Diaz, NCBI - National Center for Biotechnology Information, "US veterans and their unique issues: enhancing health care professional awareness". www.ncbi.nlm.nih.gov/pmc/articles/PMC4671760/

See also: Randy S. Roth, "Pain in Combat Veterans Returning from the Wars in Iraq and Afghanistan", https://www.michigan.gov/documents/lara/R._Roth-Pain_in_Combat_Veterans_2_368094_7.pdf

* * *

Veterans at Post World War Two Harvard

When my father matriculated to Harvard in 1945, he told me of the rift that existed between the returning veterans to campus and the fresh faced eighteen-year olds that came to Harvard straight out of high school. Not only were the veterans often five to six years older, but they had often suffered terribly, had gruesome injuries and some probably had would be called PTSD, or Post Traumatic Stress Disorder. In World War One, in which my grandfather fought, they called it "shell shock", but in any case, there was a cultural divide between the two groups. Nevertheless, one public support of WW2 was great enough that I imagine veterans were treated well, which must have had some positive health effects.

Today, veterans return to a country where good jobs are scarce and there are few positive places to go to. However, some colleges are classified as "veteran friendly", and there are websites that rate how "veteran friendly" colleges are or are not. What I saw on the various websites was mostly reference to the following:

- *tuition breaks*
- *lounges for veterans only*
- *a counselor to talk to*
- *wellness checks*
- *events for veterans to mingle*

Part of my work in the time to come is to learn about steps taken to support vets on campus that I have failed to identify.

Veteran Friendly College Websites

I looked at the six different media outlets below and typed in "military friendly". What I reported in the previous question is what I found. Perhaps more in depth research would reveal more good work that campus veteran's centers are doing.

newenglandcollegeonline.com
militarybenefits.info
bestcolleges.com
bestvalueschools.com
study.com
lendedu.com

181. What is one dangerous thought that I hope to get out of the head of veterans that suffer terribly? That they have nothing to offer and that there are too many people anyway. I hear it again and again; "there are too many people", and the fact is that this is a partial truth. Yes, there are too many cars on the roads, and I understand the feeling of wishing that there were fewer.

That said, one proper response to "too many people" is to through better "Green Plans" at schools and colleges, which is one reason the subject is addressed in questions 86-110. For the record, the three areas to work on, or the "Big Three" as I call them, are; fighting animal cruelty, more emphasis on conservation and reversing species extinction. I don't just believe that veterans could enjoy these steps forward like everyone else, they could be a critical component of making these things happen on campus. This mentality is not just a boost in the value at regional/ community colleges, but in making them places of healing, growth and opportunity.

182. How is Derrick Z. Jackson's article in The Boston Globe on community colleges a resource for both community college advocates and veterans? In the September 3rd, 2015 article "If a College Had an Extra 200 Million Dollars", Jackson succeeded in getting community college presidents to explain how they would use additional funding. Ideally, we might use this feedback to help figure out veterans can utilize these colleges to gain skills and employment, while responding to the region´s need for skilled workers.

In the article, Jackson also points out that a donation of $400 million to Harvard was larger than the annual budget for all of the Massachusetts community colleges. In the article you can see how the presidents of those colleges said they would spend additional funding of the size Harvard received. (9)

Serve Veterans, Serve Adults It is my opinion that effective responses to the feedback of these presidents in serving veterans is that it can also be used to better serve adult students. Why? It is my opinion that veterans and adults are more likely to be looking for education or training that will lead to employment.

183. What are some things to keep in mind with regard to the effective integration of veterans into manufacturing through community colleges? The number one point is that veterans will need someone to help them figure out how their skills from the military can be applied in the workforce, and perhaps Veteran's Centers can help with that. To surf existing programming, community college website visitors can either go to the sites of individual colleges, or to the state portals, to see the whole system, which are on page 7.

• *First Quote on Manufacturing* The most influential quote on manufacturing in this book was by the president of the University of Massachusetts at Lowell, in which she pointed out that we as a nation were at risk of losing 3 million jobs in manufacturing.

• *Second Quote on Manufacturing* The second most influential quote on manufacturing was by Jennifer McNelly of The Manufacturing Institute, when she said "80% of manufacturers report having a hard time finding quality workers. At the same time, we have a million veterans coming home over the next four years."

• *MassDevelopment* At the high school level, the AMPitUp! method of making videos to promote local manufacturers is educational and supports the companies and jobs that will be a a soft landing for graduates.

Perhaps as a result of "being the labor force solution for Vermont", Vermont Technical College was able to get funding from the U.S. Department of Labor.

* * *

9. "If a College Had an Extra $200 Million", Derrick Jackson, The Boston Globe, September 3, 2015
* * *

184. How can the integration of practical coursework for veterans of all ages be a response to the issue of declining college enrollment in New England? It might bring in a whole new demographic of students to boost enrollment. Many think of love as the garden of the young, and many think of college and even community colleges in the same way. "It's not for us", as the father of Rudy in the movie of the same name told his son. (10) However, although it is true that playing football for Notre Dame is indeed not for most of us, and that indeed true love is often the garden of the young, we need to shift our mentality and begin to imagine how the New England public college system can best serve those who have served us.

Rethinking the Role of Community and Public Colleges

The truth of the matter is that although that shift in thinking is a large one, it is a great step forward in and of itself. Once we have shifted our mentality, we can begin to see new possibilities. In short, these colleges can support vets through:

- Apprenticeships
- Manufacturing training (MEP)
  Manufacturing Extension Partnership
- Address the lack of skilled labor
- Be a healthy community support
- Allow vets access to high quality food on campus
- Offer business opportunities
- Allow the opportunity to participate in CSAs
- Lead in language programs
- Be an access point to community radio

Utilizing Existing Campus Resources

I emphasize that we learn about how veterans can utilize existing resources on campus before talking about new roles, and I found a video by Bunker Hill Community College helpful with the basics. (11) Boosting the role of veteran's centers may require new funding, but that is one of the reasons this book advocates for funding of community and public colleges, because the process of retooling the skills of veterans advocates may require new training and support.

* * *

10. Rudy is a 1993 sports film directed by David Anspaugh.
11. Raul Fernandez, Student Veterans Testimonial, Bunker Hill Community College video. www.youtube.com/watch?v=3JphB4o4Tuc

* * *

126

185. Why was reading an article by the president of Tulane University a bitter but ulimately welcome reality check? Just when I thought that I had gotten a handle on much of the innovation happening in education, I came across his article, and I realized that I was only aware of a small percentage of it. The article contains both good news and bad news though; the good news is that there is a great deal of innovation to learn about, but the bad news is that these smaller, highly innovative colleges threaten the larger, more established ones. However, it's better for the larger colleges to be aware of this, and begin responding to it, which is a task I believe they can handle.

"The emerging story of our colleges and universities is fundamentally one of hope, with courageous leaders spearheading a culture of innovation and inspirational models offering the promise of a brighter future for our youth, and hence our nation".

See: "How Smaller Colleges are Disrupting Higher Education", by Mike Fitts. Knowledge@wharton, May 31, 2018. **See:** http://knowledge.wharton.upenn.edu/article/smaller-colleges-disrupting-higher-education/

186. What was another point on innovation that could be applied to veterans? The main point of the article above was abundantly clear; "innovate or die". The simple truth is we need to figure out how to best serve veterans and damaged combat veterans at public colleges. A few ideas put forward included:

• *a college president that turned the football field into a working farm*
• *the choice of Amherst College to move away from loans to financial aid*
• *expression of the need to create a system of urban "work colleges"*

Adapting is also especially hard for older veterans, who might think they don't belong on campus or that they couldn't make the adjustment. In fact, the quote above from Tulane president Mike Fitts about "our youth", is in and of itself something to think about. To best serve all kinds of veterans, we're going to need to explore all kinds of ideas, and perhaps that process will help us adapt to older students, some of whom may be looking for more practical programming. (12)

187. How can on campus CSAs work to connect veteran students to the food they need to build health? The same way that CSAs can help anyone else. The ultimate goal is that some vets might have a relationship with their local farmer, although the first step is just to get fed by them. Beyond the tactics to achieve this outlined in Table 7, if community colleges were to commit to buying a certain amount of food locally, vets enrolled in a class or classes could then benefit. (13)

* * *

12. "How Smaller Colleges are Disrupting Higher Education", Knowledge@wharton, May 31, 2018, http://knowledge.wharton.upenn.edu/
13. '"About Our CSA Membership", Stockbridge School of Agriculture, UMass Amherst, https://stockbridge.cns.umass.edu/csa-membership
* * *

Stockbridge On-Campus CSA - Community Supported Agriculture

One existing example of an on-campus CSA in New England is the Stockbridge School of Agriculture at the University of Massachusetts at Amherst, whereby students are able to purchase farm shares and pick them up at the Farm Stand through the Student Farm CSA (14). What that means is local agriculture is supported and students and faculty can get affordable, healthy produce. This is one of those programs veteran's centers might be able to explain to new or prospective veteran students.

188. How is the Boston Public Market a good business model? Whereas students can get access to food through the CSA, the BPM model is good because farmers can sell produce to the public with small overhead costs.

Veteran-Student Access to Boston Public Market Style Booths

This book promotes the Boston Public Market model (15) for creating farm jobs, as it is the first year round farmer's market in New England. The existence of the market means veterans in the area can pick up healthy produce at an affordable price. It is also a response to the trend of shopping online, because as a result vendors sharing space, they drastically cut overhead, and small businesses become viable. The question is; might veterans associated with community colleges participate in any business opportunities from this arrangement? After all, having use of the booth to sell their farm products or working for someone else's booth might be a way for them to get their own business started.

One of the main things I noticed while walking around the BPM in Boston was how highly specialized some of the booths were. That's to say that some of the vendors such as Siena Farms, (16) had a wide variety of produce just like any good sized farm, but some of the booths were highly specialized, selling just one product that they were able to grow in a very limited space.

189. What is a freight farm and how can they be a connect between New England schools and veterans? For starters, a "freight farm" is a farm that operates in a shipping container, and which uses a hydroponic method for watering and artifical sunlight. To get both a visual and good explanation of how they work, you can watch the video on youtube about the freight farm at the University of Massachusetts at Dartmouth, where the crops are served at the school cafeteria.

* * *

14. Ibid.

15. "The Boston Public Market is an indoor, year-round marketplace featuring 35 New England artisans and food producers housed under one roof offering fresh foods, prepared meals, crafts, and specialty items. Residents and visitors alike can find seasonal, locally sourced food from Massachusetts and New England, including fresh produce, meat and poultry, eggs, dairy, seafood, baked goods, specialty items, crafts, and prepared breakfast, lunch, and dinner options. Everything sold at the Market is produced or originates in New England."

wwwbostonpublicmarket.org/about

16. Siena Farms CSA, https://sienafarms.com/csa/
* * *

128

Another such "small space" farm at the high school level is the "freight farm" at the Boston Latin School. (17) However, the freight farm at Boston Latin is only one of many such "farms" in New England; learning about others and how their success might be duplicated as a model of Small Businesses for Veterans.

Including Veteran Students If we see an increase in the number of these shared space markets and freight farms, these locations might serve as a reconnect for the demographic that New England colleges need to recognize as potential future students; both the veterans currently at home and the forty thousand or so coming home in the next ten years. If I hear about a wounded veteran that is selling the food he grows at a booth at a community college farm, I'm going.

See: blsleafygreenmachine.com

190. Why is the strategic location of New England community colleges so important to those who need community? As you can see on page seventy two, they are all located in different parts of Massachusetts, and in fact you can be anywhere in the state without being too far from one. This is the same anywhere in New England, although to be sure the distances are greater in the northern states. In fact, this is clearly why I saw them referred to as "regional colleges" on the website of a Vermont college. So, although programming that leads to employment certainly boosts the value of these colleges, so too is making them truly welcoming places.

Safe Spaces are Good and So Are Awesome Communities

Today we often hear derogatory talk of "safe spaces", and the term becomes so politicized that we lose sight of the tremendous importance and need for safe places for people to go, whether they are someone who is picked on or whether they need a place to heal. It's with that in mind that I emphasize here the value that community and public colleges can provide. Many of us have seen the movie An Officer and a Gentleman, (18) when Richard Gere (Zack Mayo) screams at the drill sergeant "I've got nowhere else to go!, I've got nowhere else to go!". However, as much as people make fun of that scene, it's also important to remember that that is the case for many veterans, especially those that suffer from severe injuries.

"For those of us who are financially insecure, who worry about their health, and never found true friends, the need for security, safety and community are real." (19)

So, when I hear talk of "safe spaces" and the extremely limited manner in which they are discussed, I grab onto it and hang a left, and ask my readers to imagine communities that respond to Gina Barrega's quote in *The Boston Herald* above. With many stressed and New England colleges going out of business left and right, it may be that safe campuses are part of the new, succesful business model.

* * *

17. Boston Latin School Freight Farm to School. www.blsleafygreenmachine.org/about-us
18. I Got Nowhere Else to Go! - An Officer and a Gentleman, (4/6) Movie CLIP (1982) HD. www.youtube.com/watch?v=6g2JN2PrHJg
19. Gina Barrega in The Boston Herald

* * *

191. What is a seldom heard perspective on how nursing and medical programs might best respond to the needs of veterans? In the paper titled "US Veterans and their Unique Issues: Enhancing Health Care Professional Awareness", a group of researchers suggested that nursing coursework include best practices for treating veterans with chronic pain, with courses that focused on it. This is clearly something that some of the great New England nursing programs, such as Salem State, might be aware of, although I have not asked them. Either way, people whose place it is to support best practices for dealing with veterans might choose to do so in such a way that veterans benefit.

What I have experienced personally is a veteran that used to shop at a second hand store, who would behave a little erratically. The shop managers suggested he was a problem customer, and although they have to have their standards in the store, the truth is that he had traumatic brain injury, or TBI, and he really couldn't help it. As it happens, I have watched videos of explosions in Iraq and Afghanistan, and the truth is that these small bombs are quite literally "not my grandfather's bombs", as the Humvee rocked in the explosion I saw looked like a small speck compared to the magnitude of a blast that must have devastating effects on the human brain.

In summary, New England colleges might consider not just exploring the ways outlined in this chapter to create opportunities for veterans, but also listening to those that wrote the paper on curriculum for doctors and nurses serving veterans. (20)

192. How can an increase in the effectiveness of colleges providing pipelines to jobs merge with the health benefits and in turn with the mission of veteran centers on campus? If we use our heads, communicate and work together, the combination of these benefits for veteran students could multiply.

Job Pipelines at Community Colleges

Veteran's centers might make returning veterans aware of job opportunities at community colleges, but maybe they need time and support to do so effectively, which is just one more reason I am glad I chose to include Derrick Z. Jackson's article from *The Boston Globe* on community college support. We are flooded with information, but not always the information we need.

One example of good jobs not being filled was in a May 15, 2018 article in *Seacoast Online*, which outlined the problem the Kittery Shipyard was having finding workers, despite the fact the jobs paid 18-24 dollars an hour to start. The article was well-written, outlined many of the points described in this book, and echoed a sentiment of slight confusion on the part of the shipyard as to why such well-paying jobs were being overlooked. The question then becomes; how to raise awareness of the training needed for these jobs that they reach veterans desperate for opportunities.

* * *

20. Maria Olenick, Monica Flowers, Valerie J. Diaz, NCBI - National Center for Biotechnology Information, "US veterans and their unique issues: enhancing health care professional awareness". www.ncbi.nlm.nih.gov/pmc/articles/PMC4671760/
* * *

Great Bay Community College (NH) Apprenticeships

"The shipyard has two apprenticeship programs: the four-year Trades Apprenticeship program administered jointly by Great Bay Community College and York County Community College, and the Worker Skills Progression program, a five-year program. SSA chairman John Joyal said while those programs see strong numbers, interest in the trades needs to be fostered earlier, among high schools, parents and guidance counselors, for example". (21)

Great Bay Community College in New Hampshire offers a program by which students can take five courses and be ready for work in the Kittery Shipyard, which seems like a program that could work very well for veterans. However, it may be that many of them simply are not aware of these jobs, not to mention that many have physical and mental handicaps to deal with. (22) Table 9 on page 85 and the associated questions on community college coursework is relevant to veterans. With constant changes and new opportunities arising, veteran's centers need to be able to identify opportunities such as those at the Kittery Shipyard. Not everyone reads the *Seacoast Online,* and so someone needs to connect this information to veterans.

For a list of twenty or so different models of apprenticeships in New England, many of which are offered through community colleges, see page eighty-nine.

193. What do we need to be aware of with regards to Manufacuring Extension Partnership trainings? I love the fact that MEP trainings can get students ready for basic manufacturing work in eight weeks and 280 hours of training, but many colleges don't have the equipment to do the trainings. In fact, a representative from the Massachusetts MEP told me that the University of Massachusetts at Lowell and Worcester Polytechnic Institute were the only two colleges in Massachusetts with the equipment to do the Computer Numerical Control (CNC) training.

194. Apart from the obvious practical benefits, how can being part of a school and community help with sharing and reaching health goals? As I learned from closely studying a doctor for the Rushey Green Time Bank in England, in which people over fifty did both service exchanges and held community events, having someone to set and reach health goals with is incredibly helpful. At a time when people lack enough quality relationships based on trust, time banking is one way to help create those relationships, but ideally being enrolled in a college is another way to do so. The story of time banks could be the subject of another book, but the point here is to ask how schools might help veterans get the benefits of such relationships.

* * *

21. "Seacoast Shipyard Association Seeks to Assure Future Workers", Seacoast Online. www.seacoastonline.com/news/20180505/seacoast-shipyard-association-looks-to-assure-future-workforce
22. "Apprenticeship NH tour starts at Great Bay Community College", February 24, 2018, Seacoast Online. www.seacoastonline.com/

* * *

School Farming and 1,000 Days of Progress

I should also say that I would love to see older veterans do better than just get their food and medicine. Those two things are awesome and should be celebrated, but veterans deserve more than that. Colleges are often regarded as the garden of the young, so we need to use our brains to help out new veteran students a bit. One step is for older veteran students to be eligible to connecting to CSA programs like that at the University of Massachusetts Stockbridge campus. (23) A second step is for student veterans to be eligible to sell any food they grow at the school farmer's markets, as one farm in Connecticut does.

195. Are any colleges responding to the need for skilled workers and enable manufacturers to create jobs in urban centers in New England? One expert on that is Jack Healy of the Massachusetts MEP, whose youtube video "Shop Talk"on the past and present of Massachusetts manufacturing, put out by the *Worcester Business Journal*, c. (24)

Urban Manufacturing and Veterans

Campuses might find a way to respond to the ultimate challenge; how to bring manufacturing to more urban areas. After all, being a veteran with PTSD in the countryside is one thing, but in urban centers it is quite another with the traffic, high costs and other stresses. To succeed in bringing manufacturing jobs to urban centers or within a train ride from them would be a great accomplishment.

Manufacturing Then and Now In the 1800's, many of the cities of Boston's north shore had a flourishing era of manufacturing, one which continued up to at least the memory of the past generation. Even during the 1940's, while one of my uncles was down in Texas working for the Army, another worked away at a factory on Bridge St. in Salem. My grandfather was a foreman there, and he made sure he always had a job at the factory, and I know my uncle appreciated it. However, it's really not that simple now; much of the manufacturing is gone and the days of parents in a foreman position being able to get a family member a job may be largely over.

Access to Meds Let's keep it real; when people need their meds they need their meds, and we need to avoid a common, worst case scenario, which is older people having to choose between food or medicine. What that means is that college campuses might offer utterly practical courses on health care, including courses on choosing the right health care plan. As is noted on page 78-79, many college courses like to compare the health care delivery systems of different countries, although it might help vets to do comparisons of the health care systems of different states, such as Massachusetts, Maine and New Hampshire, for example.

* * *

23. "About Our CSA Membership", Stockbridge School of Agriculture, UMass Amherst, https://stockbridge.cns.umass.edu/csa-membership
24. Jack Healy, Youtube Video: "Shop Talk". *Worcester Business Journal*
* * *

197. With declining enrollment at many colleges, why are veterans a good, new demographic to attract? According to an article in *Forbes; "highly selective admission universities' enrollments are at an all time high and their problem is not attracting students but deciding who to turn away"*. That article goes on to say that; "the gap between the wealthier top and and usually poorer bottom schools is widening sharply". So, the issue of declining enrollment is not felt everywhere, but only at some schools, which is an important point to remember. (25)

See: Richard Vedder, "Why Enrollment is Shrinking at Many American Colleges", *Forbes*, July 5, 2018.

According to an article in *Inside Higher Ed*, the enrollment declines are steepest in the Northeast and Midwest. In fact, that was the title of the article; "Enrollment Declines Steepest in Midwest and Northeast". There have been six straight years in which college enrollment has declined in the U.S. Additionally, according to an article by Jill Barshay, the number of college students in all six New England states is predicted to decline by more than 15% after 2025.

So, it seems that 40,000 veterans coming home to NE in the next 10 years is an opportunity for colleges, if they can design coursework and a campus experience interesting enough to attract both younger or older veterans.

198. Why is The Boston College Veteran Softball Game a great model of connecting schools with veterans? It is a win-win for everyone. While doing The New England College Sports Show on 91.7 FM (26), I took note of the work of *Team Impact* and some efforts to reduce concussions. However, with with regards to veterans, I was impressed by the Boston College Veteran's softball game, in which the BC baseball team hosts a softball game in which the teams of players and veterans play together. It is a breath of fresh of air for everyone involved. A vet noted that a number of veterans started comparing notes with each other, and that they began to form friendships, which in some cases became symbiotic. (27)

199. What is the potential value of veterans to supporting so-called "campus green plans"? Their presence might help a more practical approach. After studying the "green plans" of many colleges in New England, I noticed the absence of adequate steps in three major categories; conservation, reduction of animal cruelty and species conservation. That's to say that I saw language in the campus "green plans" on the subject of animal cruelty, but I found it inadequate to have a significant enough impact on the suffering of "food animals". In the case of reversing species extinction, the language was non existent.

* * *

25. Richard Vedder, "Why Enrollment is Shrinking at Many American Colleges", Forbes, July 5, 2018.
26. 91.7 FM, WMWM is a broadcast service of Salem State University with a long and storied history.
27. Youtube Video: "Boston College Veterans Softball game"
* * *

It seems to me that just as the war grizzled veterans that returned to the Harvard campus after World War Two were of an utterly different mentality than the fresh faced students that went straight to college out of high school, so too might the attitude of veterans be different when it comes to both suffering and the incredible opportunities that a visit to national parks can bring.

The "CPR" and the Lessons of Katahdin "CPR" is a term coined for this book, and is the "conservation participation rate", or the percentage of Americans that participate in conservation. In short, the tone surrounding the creation of the 68,000 acre national monument in Maine was, in my opinion, a lost opportunity to engage the public in what should have been a cathartic discussion on preserving our natural resources. If we do decide to replace the dysfunctional conversations with discussion of the opportunities new parks represent when discussing the subject of Maine North Woods(28), let's think about how to engage vets in that discussion.

The Top Five New National Parks *Travelers Magazine* published a list of the five best posssible new national parks. The role veterans can play in being a part of conservation is simple: the next time a new park is proposed, veteran science class members might be able to contribute, so we can do better than we did when talking about Katahdin. A video on the reasons for a new national park in Maine was by a woman from the group *North Woods,* called "The Heart of the Proposed Maine Woods National Park", by Lee Ann Szelog. In that video, she emphasized the importance of protecting the wilds of northern Maine through the creation of a new national park there. Perhaps voices of veteran students can add to the conversation.

200. What is a reality with regard to veterans coming home and opportunities in manufacturing? Two million female veterans are currently in the U.S., and starting in 2018, 200,000 female veterans began to come back to the U.S. from service overseas, and of course many of them will be looking for work. This comes at the same time as 80% of manufacturers report difficulty finding quality workers. Many of us have somehow gotten the impression that there aren't any opportunities in manufacturing, or at least are unaware of them. In the words of one Marine:

"Veterans are certainly a stable force within any workplace".

Youtube video: "A Future for Veterans in Manufacturing".

"The whole cycle of improvement in the military in my mind was driven by the people doing the work. The whole cycle of improvement on the manufacturing floor is driven by the people doing the manufacturing."

Paula Kilrain, U.S. Navy Veteran (29)

* * *

28. Lee Ann Szelog, Youtube Video: "The Heart of the Proposed Maine Woods National Park".
29. *Arconic* Youtube video: "Women Veterans: Military to Manufacturing" produced by the Manufacturing institute and Arconic Foundation.

* * *

201. Why might it make sense for veterans with mechanical or engineering experience to know about the manufacturing centers in New England? If veterans return to the U.S. and wanted to apply what they learned here in manufacturing, then they should know that two of the greatest support systems of manufacturers are the Advanced Manufacturing centers at the University of Maine and the University of New Hampshire. Ideally, veterans in New England will see how these two centers might help them utilize pre-existing knowlege to reach their goals.

War Experiences as Experience for Peacetime I am influenced by the experience of my grandfather in World War 1, which radically altered his work life after. Born in 1890, he had graduated from the University of Wisconsin a few years previous when he shipped of to war in 1917, as part of the equivalent of what is now known as the Army Corps of Engineers. Although only in his late twenties during the war, he took part in projects that gave him experience he never would have gotten outside of the military during wartime. Today's veterans can be useful in supporting the mission of The John Olson Advanced Manufacturing Center, which seeks to;

1. modernize traditional manufacturing technologies
2. advance and create new high efficiency state of the art materials and technologies
3. address the skills gap in US manufacturing, and
4. serve as a conduit for students and industry to the next generation of manufacturing technologies". (30) (John Olson)

The University of Maine Advanced Manufacturing Center

The key takeaways I found on the Maine AMC site was "the center maintains an investigate develop design build approach to to providing engineering and manufacturing solutions. The AMC's purpose and core compentency exist in; engineering, research, manufacturing and support services". If you go on their website, you can see the subcategories and how they support the four core competencies.

202. How do New England schools with manufacturing programs cater to veterans? This is the big question, because it seems that many Americans are relatively unaware of the resurgence in manufacturing, and do not know how to take advantage of those opportunities. Those two realities are part of the reason for this book. Veteran's centers on campus are one resource, but if we are going to effectively connect veterans to manufacturing programs that lead to employment, we need to think about that. This needs to happen both for the million that have come home or are coming home in the years to come, including about 40,000 to New England.

* * *

30. The Advanced Manufacturing Center at the University of Maine is responding to the needs of manufacturers and people looking for a career. "The core mission of the center is to assist manufacturers reach their goals. The core strategies of the AMC are; engineering, research, manufacturing and support services, and to serve as a pipeline for trained, skilled workers who will be able to successfully step into the state's manufacturing sector with practical knowledge and experience." https://umaine. edu/amc/about/

* * *

203. What are some examples of jobs that need to be filled that vets having a hard time physically or mentally could handle? I think the truth is that aren't that many of them, but as we get the New England economy going, as I believe we will, I think more jobs which leads me to what I call "chill out jobs". That is, jobs with few complications, but rather only a task to perform. The best example of a job like that is the story a friend told me about the night shift at Stop n' Shop. This friend was looking for a job, but not a career, and not the stress that comes with so many other positions. I believe he started out at about twelve dollars an hour, but got up to about fourteen, which worked out well, because he worked about fifty hours a week and lived with his mother.

Hopefully, as we get New England agriculture and manufacturing going, making that list will become easier, and veterans returning home will have more options to transition into.

204. What are some examples of morning rituals or community activities at schools that veterans might enjoy particularly? I choose to start by saying that I sense many veterans might enjoy some of these communal activities especially, in part because of a greater need for community, and in part because of either visible or invisible wounds that need healing.

Rise and Shine However, the best early morning assembly I ever took part in was not in school, and not even in New England, but on the campus of Colorado St. university, where I was part of a gathering of the Swedish churches in the U.S. Every morning, we used to sing "Rise and Shine", and it was epic. There were 4,000 of us, it was co-ed, and I have not experienced anything like it since.

College of the Atlantic Color Out The Bar Harbor, Maine college is fairly unique in that they only offer one major, human ecology, which is the study of the effect of the humans on the planet. Their annual Color Out event looks like a blast.

205. What is an opportunity in conservation biology for New England programs looking to attract new students? One dimension of conservation and education is the ongoing issues of animals going extinct, and how schools can respond to this. And, in my mind I ask if veterans on campus might help with this. As Lucas Moyer-Horner wrote in his 2010 *PubMed* article;

"Conservation biology courses, taught worldwide at universities, typically focus on the proximal causes of extinction without teaching students how to respond to this crisis".

For teachers that wanted to talk about animal extinctions, a useful little guide is called *Threatened Animals Worldwide: A Folding Pocket Guide to Familiar Species*. It features photos of the threatened animals, with some of the causes, as well as what could be called "next steps". One could base a whole course on this little publication, and maybe doing so attracted new veteran customers to college campuses.

136

206. What is one course vets and everyone can benefit from in the post COVID-19 era? The University of Texas offers a course on "Maximizing Social Security" that runs through every aspect of applying for and maximizing Social Security. For starters, there are eighty-one different pathways to benefits, among countless other things to know. (31) The general population learning to maximize their Social Security benefits may seem five degrees of separation away from keeping restaurants, farms, and small businesses afloat, but as Brockton Mayor Robert Sullivan said;

"We need anything and everything that helps keep them afloat" (32)

* * *

31. University of Texas Extended Campus, https://informalutexas.edu/classes/maximizing-social-security
32. Lisa Kashinsky, "More Economic Aid Sought: Walsh and Up to 50 Municipal Leaders Push State to Help Struggling Businesses", Boston Herald, 21, December 20, 2020.

* * *

207 to 215
Veterans and College Sports

"There's no way you can go over there (deployed overseas) for a year and not be different....you get so used to everything being life and death. I felt so old."

Justine Bottorf, Rower, Age 23, University at Buffalo, SUNY (1)

207. How can veterans playing college sports be good for them, the school they attend, the team they play for and everyone else? Just as veterans have a great deal to contribute to college campuses as a whole, they have a great deal to bring to sports teams. In fact, experience in the military can be particularly valuable to a team. The quote from from Justine Bottorf because hers is indeed a story seldom told. I also like it because it shows that the culture on campus in post World War Two Harvard and today are not so different; people of radically different backgrounds had a hard time communicating then, and still do now.

208. What is an organization that connects veterans with college teams that more people need to know about? That would be Athletes of Valor, an organization that was founded by a Massachusetts native. The organization needs to exist to educate vets about eligibility that too many vets don't know they have.

Eligibility Many veterans don't know that they are eligible for college sports, because NCAA rules dictate that students have five years after high school graduation to play. However, the NCAA also grants waivers for those who have been in active service in the military. So, a veteran that went into the military out of high school and served for seven years might think that at age twenty-five, his days of playing college sports are a bygone dream, but that's not necessarily the case.

Graduation Rates Whereas most student athletes have an extremely high graduation rate of 85%, veteran student graduation rates lag behind at 50%. (2) Many veteran students feel a void that can't be filled by much of the programming of traditional coursework; they miss the sense of honor and team. This is precisely why playing sports can be so helpful.

Coaches Love Veteran Players Veteran athletes tend be more matured, disciplined and team-oriented than younger players that have not served. As the football coach at the University of Central Florida said; *"If you want to see an example of*

* * *

1. Douglas A. Wissing, University at Buffalo, SUNY. "Battlefield to Homefield: Veterans Returning from War find a New Team, and a Different Kind of Camaraderie", NCAA. www.ncaa.org/static/champion/battlefield-to-home-field/
2. Griffin Mahoney, "College Sports After The Military", Athletes of Valor, July 25, 2017. www.athletesofvalor.com/articles/playing-college-sports-after-the-military
* * *

a man of sacrifice and character, then you don't have to look any further than Rory Coleman." (3) Athletes of Valor has a very ambitious goal, which is to have one veteran playing a sport at every single college across the country. The impact that reaching that goal would have is something I need to think about.

See: athletesofvalor.org (4)

209. What is Team Impact and why should you know about it? *Team Impact,* a group that pairs children with life threatening and debilitating diseases with college sports teams. (5) Children become full members of the team, complete with a locker and seat at the dining room table. ESPN once called "The Kinnick Wave" out at the University of Iowa "the coolest new tradition in college sports", (6) but I would argue that the approach of *Team Impact* is more impactful. After all, *Team Impact* creates a full support system for families that otherwise would be fighting all alone.

"Team Impact is something that parents dream of for their children".

A good way to begin to learn about the group is to go to their website and watch the video there. Anoor to look at teams that participate in the program.

How It Impacts Veteran Athletes If *Athletes of Valor* is indeed successful in reaching its goal of *"having one veteran on one team at every college in the country",* then there would be a chance that teams would have a veteran that could participate in the support system for the kid fighting for his or her life. Not only does that mean that the veteran could be a role model for his or her team, but that the team itself would be stronger and possibly even more powerful in the support of the whole family. If it was a veteran such as Rory Coleman that had experienced serious injury, then the connection to and support of the parents could be strong!

See: *goteamimpact.org*

210. Why might a revival of college radio be of particular value to veterans that desperately need community? Because one of the best ways to listen to college radio is to listen to it with fellow students, and I think that veterans might enjoy that particularly. It's mentioned earlier in this book that 90.3, WZBC used to pipe the channel into The Eagles Nest, a common area, so students could all listen together. (7) Despite being in the age of cell phones, could still be done. After all, most have headphones for their devices, so a broadcast to a common area wouldn't prevent private listening. This is something older students and veterans might especially enjoy, as one of the most difficult things for veterans is to integrate into campus.

* * *

3. Youtube Video, "Service Came before College Football for UCF's Rory Coleman", College Game Day, ESPN.
4. You Tube Video, "Athletes of Valor".
5. Team Impact, http://www.goteamimpact.org/
6. Team Impact Hype Video:
www.youtube.com/watch?time_continue=58&v=ODOL6m6K28Y
7. "WZBC-NEWTON 90.3 FM", WVBC, https://www.wzbc.org/wvbc
* * *

211. How many college radio stations are there in New England? There are about fifty college radio stations in New England, and an interesting survey would be to find out how many of those broadcast into a common space. Also interesting survey would be to find out how many used to broadcast into a common area, and how many do now. I imagine there is a huge difference between, the 1970's and now. (8)

Doing a survey of whether or not college radio stations broadcast on campus would be hard, although the "Top 25 College Radio Stations" would be a place to start. With Boston University's WTBU at number 14 and Emerson's WERS, 88.9 at number 25 on that list, a start is to find out what those stations do.

Whether we are talking about college radio, intramural sports or anything else, communal activities are going to have a greater positive impact on those that have a hard time integrating, such as veterans dealing with PTSD, Traumatic Brain Injury or whatever else. Reestablishing college radio in this way is just one step that would be especially good for veterans, but also the entire community.

212. How might a shift in attitude toward college sports and college sports event planning be good for veteran students and their families? By a shift in attitude I mean a shift toward appreciating the simple joy and values of amateur sports, and veterans with great attitudes can help with that.

Affordability: College Sports I feel bad for parents of young people that are dying to go to pro games, especially when the parents really can't afford it, and so I started down the road of promoting college sports events. Although having a physical "play space" is tough to find at big time college games in New England, maybe it's worth it for parents to look into that, and even pack (balls, gloves or lacrosse sticks) accordingly.

Role Models and the Participation Rate Athletes can be great role models for younger athletes. Some colleges also struggle with the "participation rate" on campus, but vets doing sports might help with that. Some schools track what they call the participation rate, and it is a very telling statistic.

213. What is the role of community college sports conferences in New England and how might veteran students benefit from and contribute to them? These conferences represent accessible vehicles for potential students to reach their goals. Two major community college athletic conferences in New England are the Yankee Small College Conference and The Massachusetts Community College Athletic conference.

"For decades, the state's community college system has helped save legions of vulnerable young men and women from the dangers of the streets and the limitations of life without higher education. Now, community college sports in Massachusetts may themselves be at risk." (9)

As inspiring as the stories of veterans playing big-time college sports are, there are also great stories to be made in sports at the community colleges. This is a lesson I learned while doing *The New England College Sports Show* on WMWM, 91.7 FM. (11) I realized during an interview with a Massachusetts state college basketball coach that community college sports leagues are often overlooked, but are also an area of opportunity.

* * *

8. "The 25 Best College Radio Stations", Pigeons and Planes, March 19, 2013, https://pigeonsandplanes.com
9. Zolan Kanno-Youngs, "Community College Sports an Endangered but Essential Species", The Boston Globe, https://www.bostonglobe.com/sports/2015/07/06/
* * *

214. How might veterans go about learning about the opportunities in Intramural sports? Two ways are to learn about the intramural league website for sign ups and "Rec it" app. The untapped potential of quality intramural to help out veterans is huge, and is also interesting because sometimes rarer sports are represented within these leagues. I also know from personal experience these teams can be highly inclusive. the "Guidebook" app can help with other programming. According to the website of one college:

"Intramurals alone attracts 35% of the student population".

A. *Intramurals Sign up*: www.imleagues.com/spa/account/registration
B. *The Rec It App:* www.imleagues.com/MobileApps.aspx
C. *The Guidebook App*

215. What are examples of how a veteran or adult athlete might use community college leagues to reach their goals? Cross Country is a prime example, because the exact times, lengths and distances that Division 1 and 2 (scholarship) schools are looking for are all spelled out online, for both men and women. So, athletes can work toward those athletic goals at a community college. Success is very quantified in track and field. For example the NCAA states that a time of 16:40 in the 5k is about what a Division 1 men's team is looking for, then the athlete can work towards that at any school with a program and qualified coach.

One 2018 *Boston Herald* article told the story of a football lineman who had scholarship offers from big time college programs, but yet chose to go to New Rochelle Community College (which closed in 2019) to play, because he was able to try out all different lineman positions and develop diverse skills.

The Role of the NJCAA

After two years of college sports radio, two years of going to the website of the NCAA every day, and five years of studying the Boston sports pages, it is ironic that a principal lessons learned is how ignored community college sports are in New England. Many of those schools are under the jurisdiction of the National Junior College Athletic Association, or NJCAA. Whether or not players that developed would choose to transfer and play Division 1 or 2 sports is up to them. What is certain is that veterans that may struggle adjusting to civilian life would have a team to help them. However, the overarching question is even bigger than that; how recreational, intramural and community college sports can boost opportunties and engagement for the forty percent.

See: www.njcaaregionxxi.com

Table 16: On Campus Support of Veterans

Exploring tactics to support and engage veterans on campus is an excellent exercise to think about innovation that might ordinarily be disregarded. With one million veterans coming home in the next decade, and 40,000 of them to New England, we have to go there. A start of is to check out the "Three Doses of Reality" below. Beyond that, adapting to returning veterans is a good exercise in adapting to attract adults looking for more practical skills and knowledge.

Three Doses of Reality	A. *Derrick Z. Jackson* The article by Derrick Z. Jackson in the Boston Globe laments support of community colleges. B. Richard Vedder "Why Enrollment is Shrinking at Many American Colleges". *Forbes.* July 5, 2018. C. *Inside Higher Ed. Article Lesson* The enrollment declines at colleges are the steepest in the Midwest and Northeast.
Relevant Tables	A. The Frustrated Mom's Twelve Pack on page 107 for parents with relatively healthy veteran children. B. Table 12 explores opportunities for the disabled. C. Table 15 outlines opportunities in manufacturing.
Contributions	participating in conservation/climate change goals reducing animal cruelty reversing species extinction. becoming part of the skilled workforce participating in Dynamic Campus Veterans centers Helping Pets for Vets go mainstream Events like the Boston College Veterans Softball game Helping colleges adapt to adult students
Existing Models of Success	A. *MassBay Community College: STEM Program:* The affordable school is an excellent option for commuters. B. *Project Ground Floor* Shared ownership of housing can help vets pay a small mortgage and build capital while living in a supportive environment. The right coursework might help facilitate. C. *The Rec It App:* www.imleagues.com/MobileApps.aspx D. *Intramurals:* imleagues.com/spa/account/registration E. NJCAA Region Twenty-One

Bibliography

Aguirre, Edwin L. "MassMEP, UMass Lowell Address New Workforce Training Program", November 03, 2015.

Allen, Charlotte "The highly educated, badly paid, often abused adjunct professors", *Los Angeles Times*, December 22, 2013 L.A.Times. www.latimes.com/

American Serengeti, directed by Andy Mitchell (2010 : Montana: National Geographic Television), DVD

ASPCA, "ASPCA Releases New Data Showing Remarkable Progress for Homeless Dogs and Cats", March 10, 2017

athleticsrecruiting.com "Track and Field Scholarship and Recruiting Standards"

Bangor Daily News, "Eastern Maine Community College Enrollment at Historic High for Fourth Straight Year", October 5th 2012

Barrega, Gina "Letters to the Editor". The Boston Herald, January 8, 2018

Berman, Sheldon, Perry Davis, Ann Koufman-Frederick, and David Urion. "The Rising Costs of Special Education in Massachusetts: Causes and Effects," in Rethinking Special Education for a New Century, edited by Chester G. Finn, Jr., Andrew J. Rotherham, and Charles R. Hokanson, Jr., 183-211. Washington, DC: Thomas B. Fordham Foundation and Progressive Policy Institute, 2001. PDF.

Boston College, Global Health Perspectives at BC: www.bc.edu/offices/international/progsummer/America/ecglobalhealth11.html.

Boston Herald Video: "Massachusetts Farms Struggle to Stay Afloat". (Ottolini 2019)

bostonrealestate.com, Monthly rent, mortgage down payment and monthly costs.

Brecht, Richard "The Language Crisis in the War on Terror," The Eisenhower Institute, Gettysburg College, October 24, 2002.

Breslow, Rebecca, Commentary: "Brookline Should Take the Lead on Recess", *The Brookline Tab,* November 10, 2018

BU Statehouse Program. Mutian Qiao. "Mass Restaurant Industry is far from a full recovery, even with help".

Bureau of Labor Statistics. www.bls.gov/eag/eag.ma.htm

Byrne, Mary "North Shore Community College Pilots Free College Program", *Wicked Local Danvers,* April 20, 2017

California State L.A. "Newly Installed Stations to Charge up Electric Vehicles". calstatela.edu/univ/ppa/spotlight/archive/2011/evchargingstations.php. 6/12/11

Caplan, Laurie   MSC, Causes of Cancer in Dogs". www.helpyourdogfightcancer.com/CausesPrevention.shtml.

Catelli, Linda A., Failing at Fairness; How America's Schools Cheat Girls, "Bottom of the Ninth; Girls Physical Education and Literature".

"Case Study: Arlington, Massachusetts." Safe Routes: National Center for Safe Routes to School. Accessed May 5, 2012. www.saferoutesinfo.org/program-tools/case-study-arlington-massachusetts.

Centers for Disease Control cdc.gov/healthyyouth/physicalactivity/facts.htm.

Colorado State Journal Gisela B. Estes, Barbara Lopez-Mayhew, Marie Therese Gardner, "Writing in the Foreign Languages Department," August 1998. http://wac.colostate.edu/journal/vol9/estes.pd

Chronicle of Higher Education, The, "How These Professors Assign Their Own

Books with a Clear Concience".

CNN Money StockWatch "Can Barnes and Noble Survive", CNN Money. September 10, 2015, http://money.cnn.com/2015/09/10/investing/barnes-and-noble/.

College Choice "50 Highest Paying Careers for College Graduates". www.collegechoice.net/50-highest-paying-careers-college-graduates/

College of Wooster, Technology Brings Spanish Playwrights into the Classroom," The College of Wooster News and Events, Feb. 27, 2013. www.wooster.edu/news/releases/2013/february/spanish-311.

Cornell Waste Management Institute, accessed June 11, 2012, http://cwmi.css.cornell.edu/aboutwmi.html.

College Values Online Metrics. "Best New England College Farms".

Crockett, Lee "Overfishing 101: A Beginner's Guide to Understanding U.S. Fishery Management," The Pew Charitable Trusts, March 30, 2011.

"Crop Mobs in Vermont." University of Vermont Center for Sustainable Agriculture. March 25, 2011www.uvm.edu/sustainableagriculture/?Page=cropmob.html.

Daly, Natasha National Geographic. February 22, 2017

Davis, Molly, "Bulldogs Study Shelter Dogs during May Term," Redlands Daily Facts, May 8, 2011.

Davison, Laura Bloomberg ""Virus Could Deplete Social Security Funds by 2030, Report Says." Portland Press Herald. October 22, 2020 www.pressherald.com

Dead Poets Society, directed by Peter Weir (1989; Burbank, CA: Walt Disney Video, 1998), DVD.

Drake, Olivia "Fresh Organic Produce Grown, Sold by Wesleyan", Wesleyan University, July 11, 2018. http:/newsletter.blogs.wesleyan.edu/

Edward Moscovitch, Closing the Gap: Raising Skills to Raise Wages (Boston: MassINc., 1997)

EIS Information Center, "Ocean Wave Energy," OCS Alternative Energy and Alternate Use Programmatic, accessed June 11, 2012, http://ocsenergy.anl.gov/guide/wave/index.cfm

Erlich, Mark. "About MassINC." www.massinc.org/About/Voices/Mark-Erlich2.aspx.

Estes, Gisela B. Barbara Lopez-Mayhew, Marie Therese Gardner, "Writing in the Foreign Languages Department," August 1998, Volume 9. http://wac.colostate.edu/journal/vol9/estes.pdf

EFMR Monitoring Group,"Wind Energy: Lesson Plans and Resource Guide,", 2009, http://www.efmr.org/edu/wind2009.pdf

Fernandez, Raul, Student Veterans Testimonial, Bunker Hill Community College video. www.youtube.com/watch?v=3JphB4o4Tuc

Fidler, John "BC Alabama Football 1984", Youtube Video. www.youtube.com/watch?v=XCExyGFkysc

Finkelstein, Barbara "Maine Voices, Maine Voices; Manufacturing's Best Days Might Be Yet to Come". Portland Press Herald. November 19th, 2016

Fitts, Mike "How Smaller Colleges are Disrupting Higher Education". May 31, 2018. www.knowledge.wharton.upenn.edu/article/smaller-colleges-disrupting-higher-education/

Fitzgerald, Jay, "Worker's Skills aren't Matching Available Jobs," Boston Globe. December 15, 2013.

Forgotten Farms.Initial Release: June 4, 2016. "The challenges facing New England's dairy Farmers, who remain the backbone of the region's agriculture, are examined". Director: Dave Simonds. Screenplay: Sarah S. Gardner. Cast (Partial): Henry W. Art, Leon Corse, Carol Chenail, Winthrop Chenall, Jane Escobar, Vic Ziemba, Donald Campbell, Louis Escobar, Linwood Rhodes.

Fraser, Matthew J. "Making Walker and Bike Paths Friendly," *Salem News.* August 21, 2014.

Freyer, Felice J. "Overdose Deaths Mass Continue Surge". *The Boston Globe,* November 7, 2016

Gabriel, Danielle Douglas "Why Massachusetts is creating its own student debt counseling unit". *The Washington Post,* November 24, 2015

Geiling, Ethan, "Is Financial Education in the Schools in Decline?" CFED, April 4, 2012. http://cfed.org

George Mason College of Science "Renewable Energy Minor," accessed May 10, 2012, http://cos.gmu.edu/academics/undergraduate/minors/renewable-energy.

Goldstene, Claire "The Politics of Contingent Academic Labor," National Education Association. www.nea.org/home/53403.html

Greenwood, Arin "ASPCA reveals historic data for shelter pets: Adoptions are up, euthanasia is down". March 9, 2017, www.today.com/

Gu Larry and Alicia Zou, "Senior Capstone Class Visits Slaughterhouse," Boston Latin School *Argo.*

Harvard Crimson "Confronting Cruelty; Harvard Should Not Tolerate Unnecessary Cruelty in its Labs". January 26, 2012.

Healy, Jack Youtube Video: "Shop Talk",*Worcester Business Journal.*

Heights, The Marta Seitz Author Page

"History of the Railroad in Danvers." Danvers Rail Trail. Accessed November 13, 2011. www.danversrailtrail.org/history.htm

"How it Works." Cape Ann Time bank. Accessed December 1, 2011. www.capeanntimebanks.org/How_it_Works.html.

Huntsman, Jon. "Energy Policy." Speech, University of New Hampshire, Durham, NH, Tuesday, November 1st, 2011.

Jacobson, Kristi and Lori Silverbush. *A Place at the Table*

Jackson, Derek Z. "If Colleges Had An Extra 200 million". *The Boston Globe* 9/03/15

Jumpshell.com "Food, utilities and rent costs for Boston".

Juravich, Tom *The Future of Work in Massachusetts*

Kanno-Youngs, Zolan "Community College Sports an Endangered but Essential Species", The Boston Globe, 07/06/2015

Kashinsky, Lisa "More Economic Aid Sought: Walsh and Up to 50 Municipal Leaders Push State to Help Struggling Businesses". *Boston Herald*, page 21, December 20, 2020.

Kennedy, Louise "Mass. Public Campuses See More Hungry And Homeless Students", WBUR. January 24, 2017

Krantz, Laura "Backlog on building upkeep is mounting at state campuses", *The Boston Globe,* 05/29`17.

Krantz, Laura "Black and Latino Enrollment Plummets at Massachusetts Community Colleges". February 4, 2021. You can see other articles by L. Krantz at her muckrack.com page.

Laton, Lyndsey "Lunch Lady Rises to Teacher's Union Leader and Takes on all Comers, Bluntly", The Washington Post, August 11, 2014

146

Lafranche, Howard "US No Longer Towers Over Latin America", Christian Science Monitor. April 18, 2009

Laidler, John "Free Finance Class a Hit at Salem State." Boston.com, March 3, 2011. www.boston.com/

Le Masurier and Charles B. Corbin "Top Ten Reasons for Quality Physical Education".

Levenson, Michael "State's Public Colleges See Rise in Hunger, Homelessness". The Boston Globe, January 25, 2017

Lohr, Steve (2017, November 1). Where the STEM Jobs Are (and Where They Aren't). The New York Times. Retrieved from https://mobile.nytimes.com/2017/11/01/education/edlife/stem-jobs-industry-careers.html

Mahoney, Griffin "College Sports After The Military". Athletes of Valor. July 25, 2017

Mahoney, Kathie "MassMEP Partners with UMass Lowell to Expand Advanced CNC Training in Massachusetts"

Marquand, Barbara, "Pros and Cons of Catastrophic Health Insurance," Insurance.com, March 1, 2014

Massachusetts Community Colleges Articulation Agreements. www.masscc.org/technical-high-schools-transfer-agreements/?amp www.mass.edu"Tuition and Mandatory Fees at Massachusetts Public Colleges and Universities".

Massachusetts Department of Agricultural Resources, Agricultural Recources Facts and Statistics, Energy and Environmental Affairs.

Massachusetts General Laws Online Chapter 272, Sections 105 and 99

Mass Bay Community College "Athletics Quick Facts. www.gomassbucs.com

mass.edu "Tuittion and Mandatory Fees at Mass. Public Colleges and Universities".

Mass Grown Map "Farm Locator". massrnc.org

MassINC Sum, Andy, Neeta Fogg, Paul Harrington, Ishwar Khatiwada, Mykhaylo Trub'skyy, Sheila Palma, Gursel Aliyev, Jacqui Motroni, Alex Plotkin, Nathan Pond, and Abilasha Rao. The State of the American Dream in Massachusetts, 2002. Boston: MassINC, 2002.

MassINC. "The State of the American Dream". 1996

MassMEP http://massmep.org/ and MassMEP "Case Studies".

Mass Resources "What is Mass Health?" MassResources.org. accessed June 11, 2012. www.massresources.org/masshealth-description.html.

Mayo Clinic "Nutrition and Healthy Eating," December 3, 2011. www.mayoclinic.com/health/organic-food/NU00255.

MCAS Wikipedia: www.en.wikipedia.org/wiki/Massachusetts_Comprehensive_Assessment_System.

McClure, Nancy, "Buffalo Bill Center of the West celebrates National Bison Day with a free film." www.centerofthewest.org

Menanteau, Phillipe "Policy Measures to Support Solar Water Heating: Information, Incentives and Regulations". World Energy Council, May 2007. www.worldenergy.org/documents/solar_synthesis.pdf.

Messenger, Stephen "College in California Becomes First to Produce More Energy Than It uses," TreeHugger, June 30, 2011.

Mohl, Bruce "T Approves $10 Weekend Commuter Rail Pass," Commonwealth Magazine.

Moscovitch Edward, Closing the Gap: Raising Skills to Raise Wages (Boston: MassINC., 1997), Executive Summary

Moulton, Patricia Radio Interview with WMAC, Northeast Television

Moyer-Horner, L., PubMed,"Education as a tool for addressing the extinction crisis: moving students from understanding to action".

Nathan, Julian "College Faces Animal Abuse Claims", *The Dartmouth*

National Center for Biotechnology Information Maria Olenick, Monica Flowers, Valerie J. Diaz, NCBI -, "US veterans and their unique issues: enhancing health care professional awareness".

National Humane Education Society, "Factory Farms".

New England Farmer's Union "Land Agriculture Act of 2014".

New England Small Farm Institute "About NESFI". www.smallfarm.org/main/about_nesfi

Nichol, Polly "Shared Housing Takes Many Forms," Vermont Housing & Conservation Board. Accessed 5/5/12. www.vhcb.org/SharedHousingArticle.html.

NJCAA Region 21 "Composite Schedule." www.njcaaregionxx1.com

No Impact Man 2009. Directors; Laura Gabbert and Justin Schein. IMDb

O'Brien, Dan, *The Lowell Sun,* "UML Christens Partnership for Workforce Development" UMass Lowell. www.uml.edu/News/news-articles/2015/sun-massmep.aspx

Olenick, Maria, Monica Flowers, Valerie J. Diaz, NCBI - National Center for Biotechnology Information, "US veterans and their unique issues: enhancing health care professional awareness". www.ncbi.nlm.nih.gov/pmc/articles/PMC4671760/

Oliver, Jamie "Targeting School Food". www.jamieoliver.com/us/foundation/jamies-food-revolution/about_jamie_oliver

O'Neil, John "On Tracking and Individual Differences: A Conversation with Jeannie Oakes". October 1992. http://www.ascd.org/publications/educational-leadership/oct92/vol50/num02/On-Tracking-and-Individual-Differences@-A-Conversation-with-Jeannie-Oakes.aspx.

Paradis, Jeff "Jeff Paradis' Powerful Plea To Maine Veterans-You're F'in Worth It!," Youtube video: www.youtube.com/watch?v=jDpDZW4F9bg

PBIC Case Studies www.pedbikeinfo.org/planning/facilities_casestudies.cfm

PBS *Shelter Me; Let's Go Home.*

People's Academy, The "Vision and Mission". www.peoplesacademy.org/about

Pew Research Center Graf, N., Fry, R., & Funk, C. (2018, January 9), "7 facts about the STEM workforce".

Pomona College of Liberal Arts Language Center, University of Minnesota. https://languagecenter.cla.umn.edu/tandem/.

Princeton Review of Green Colleges "Best College Farms".

Ramos, Dante "Adjunct Professors Unionize, Revealing Deeper Malaise", Boston Globe, March 24, 2016.

Reed College Residence Life "Language Houses", www.reed.edu/res_life/on_campus/language_houses.html.

Rocheleau, Matt "Their Budgets Strained, Students Turn to Campus Food Pantries". *The Boston Globe.* December 15, 2014

Roth, Randy S. "Pain in Combat Veterans Returning from the Wars in Iraq and Afghanistan". www.michigan.gov/documents/lara/R._Roth-Pain_in_Combat_

148

Veterans_2_368094_7.pdf

Safe Routes "Using Safe Routes to School to Combat the Threat of Violence", www.saferoutespartnership.org/sites/default/files/pdf/Street-Scale-Using-Safe-Routes-to-School-to-Combat-Threat-of-Violence.pdf

Salary.com, average vocational salaries

Scarry, Joseph T., "Big Brother in Area Studies," *The Harvard Crimson*, December 5, 2003. www.thecrimson.com/

Seacoast Online, "Seacoast Shipyard Association Seeks to Assure Future Workers", May 5, 2018

Shanker, Albert, United Federation of Teachers, "Who We Are". www.uft.org/who-we-are/history/albert-shanker.

Simon, Scott "High School Newspapers: An Endangered Species". June 1, 2013

Social Security Administration "Long Term Financial Outloook". ssa.gov

Sudbury Valley Trustees "Programs"

Symonds, Bill Radio Interview with Robin Young of WBUR 90.9.

Szelog, Lee Ann Youtube Video: "The Heart of the Proposed Maine Woods National Park".

Talerico, Kate "Mercy for Animals Fellow fights for animal rights", on February 25, 2015, *The Brown Daily Herald*

Thoreau, Henry David, "The Village", Walden; or Life in the Woods". Tinkner & Field. Boston 1854

Threatened Animals Worldwide, A Familiar Pocket Guide to Familiar Species. Kavanaugh/Leung, A Waterford Discovery Book.

Tip O'Neill Congressional Papers, 1936-1994. www.library.bc.edu

Travelers Magazine "Top 5 Picks for New National Parks".

Texas, University of, Extended Campus, Course: "Maximizing Social Security", https://informalutexas.edu/classes/maximizing-social-security

Triunfo, Christian "Walsh Implements New Program to Create New Jobs", *The Huntington News*

Tsupros, N., Kohler, R., & Hallinen, J. (2009). STEM education: A project to identify the missing components. Pittsburgh, PA: Intermediate Unit 1: Center for STEM Education and Leonard Gelfand Center for Service Learning and Outreach, Carnegie Mellon University.

Tufts Daily, The "Friedman School Screens Forgotten Farms, discusses New England Dairy Farms", April 13, 2018.

University of Texas Extension School. "Maximizing Social Security"

U.S. Department of Commerce Langdon, D., McKittrick, G., Beede, D., Khan, B., & Doms, M. (2011). STEM: Good Jobs Now and for the Future. Washington, DC: Office of the Chief Economist, Economics and Statistics Administration, Retrieved from www.esa.doc.gov/sites/default/files/stemfinalyjuly14_1.pdf

U.S. Small Business Administration "Massachusetts Total Private Employment" 2019

Vedder, Richard "Why Enrollment is Shrinking at Many American Colleges", *Forbes,* July 5, 2018.

Vermont Public Radio "It's Just Really Sad: Green Mountain College Students, Faculty React to Closure". Nina Keck. January 25, 2019

Weale, Sally "Britons Should learn Polish, Punjabi and Urdu to boost social cohesion". January 18, 2017. *The Guardian.*

WBUR "Mass. Public Campuses See More Hungry And Homeless Students". January 24, 2017. www.wbur.org/

WGBH Basic Black, "Saving Bookstores". 12/6/20

Wheelock, Anne "The Case for Untracking", *Association for Supervision and Curriculum Development,* October1992. www.ascd.org/

Wissing, Douglas A. University at Buffalo, SUNY. "Battlefield to Homefield: Veterans Returning from War find a New Team, and a Different Kind of Camaraderie", NCAA. www.ncaa.org/static/champion/battlefield-to-home-field/

WMUR-TV "Many NH Farm Stands See Increase in Sales Amid Covid 19". 3/25/20.

WMWM Salem 91.7 FM "History" www.wmwmsalem.com/history

Zakaria, Fareed "Why America's obsession with STEM Education is Dangerous". *The Washington Post,* March 26, 2015.

Zawacki, Emily "Recyclemania". *The Lawrentian*

Index

www.ingramcontent.com/pod-product-compliance
Lightning Source LLC
Chambersburg PA
CBHW070806280326
41934CB00012B/3077